NEW DAD DEVOTIONAL

A 52 WEEK JOURNEY OF FAITH, GROWTH, AND FATHERHOOD

BY
ANDERS BENNETT

ADISAN Publishing AB

To :

Message :

From :

TABLE OF CONTENTS

INTRODUCTION

Welcome to one of the most terrifying and wonderful chapters of your life.

If you're reading this book, chances are someone who cares about you deeply placed it in your hands—perhaps your wife, a parent, or a friend who saw the mixture of excitement and panic in your eyes when you talked about becoming a father. They chose well. This isn't just another parenting guide filled with techniques and theories. This is a companion for the journey ahead, written for men who want to father with intention, faith, and the quiet confidence that comes from walking closely with God.

Let me be honest with you from the start: it's okay to be scared. If you weren't feeling some level of fear right now, that would be unusual. The weight of responsibility you're carrying—or about to carry—is real. You're going to shape another human being's understanding of love, security, and what it means to trust. That's both an incredible privilege and a sobering reality.

I speak from experience as a father of six children. Two came to us the traditional way, through pregnancy and birth. Four others found their way into our family through the foster care system, each carrying their own stories and needs. In every case—biological or adopted—I felt that familiar cocktail of overwhelming love mixed with the terrifying question: "What if I mess this up?"

Here's what I've learned through sleepless nights, teenage attitudes, scraped knees, graduation ceremonies, and everything in between: your fears about making mistakes aren't unfounded. You will make mistakes. Every father does. But God's grace is bigger than your worst parenting moment, and His love for your children runs deeper than any error you might make along the way.

Today, I have a daughter teaching in England, a son successful enough to travel between Canada and Sweden for work, and another daughter training to be a pastor. The other three are still writing their stories, each one unique and precious. Did I parent perfectly? I most definitely didn't. But God used imperfect love, countless prayers, and a commitment to keep learning to help shape them into the remarkable people they're becoming.

That's the heart of this devotional: not perfection, but faithfulness. Not having all the answers, but knowing where to find them. Not eliminating fear, but learning to move forward in faith despite it.

HOW TO USE THIS DEVOTIONAL

This book is designed to meet you wherever you are in your journey as a father. Whether you're still counting down weeks until your baby arrives, learning to change diapers with shaking hands, or navigating the beautiful chaos of life with a toddler, these devotions will speak to your experience.

The Structure: Each week follows the same pattern to help you build a sustainable rhythm:

- **A Key Scripture Verse** from the New Living Translation (NLT), chosen for clarity and ease of understanding during those foggy, sleep-deprived moments
- **A Real Story** that connects the biblical truth to actual fatherhood experiences
- **Biblical Reflection** that unpacks the Scripture in practical, relevant ways
- **A Simple Action Step** you can take this week—nothing overwhelming, just one small way to live out what you're learning
- **Two Reflection Questions** to help you process your thoughts and prayers
- **A Guided Prayer and Blessing** to close each week with worship and hope

Your Pace: You don't have to follow this book week by week if that doesn't work for your life. Skip around if a particular theme calls to you. Return to the weeks that especially encouraged you. The goal isn't completion; it's growth.

Your Bible: We've used the New Living Translation throughout because it communicates God's truth in clear, contemporary language. When you're operating on three hours of sleep, you need Scripture that speaks plainly to your heart without requiring a theology degree to understand.

Your Community: Consider reading this alongside other new dads, whether that's your brother-in-law, a few friends from church, or from work who are in the same season. The reflection questions work well for group discussion, and there's something powerful about discovering you're not the only one who sometimes feels overwhelmed by fatherhood.

Your Family: Some weeks include suggestions for involving your wife or even your child in the action steps. Fatherhood isn't a solo journey, and the strongest families are built when everyone grows together.

Remember, this isn't about becoming the perfect dad your child deserves—none of us will achieve that. This is about becoming the faithful dad God can use to love, guide, and bless your child. There's a significant difference, and it makes all the difference in the world.

Your child doesn't need a perfect father. They need a present one, a growing one, a praying one. They need you, walking humbly with your God and learning to love them the way your Heavenly Father loves you.

Let's begin this journey together.

Starting Strong:

Learning to see fatherhood through God‘s eyes

WEEK 1

You're Called for This

"Children are a gift from the Lord; they are a reward from him."
— Psalm 127:3 (NLT)

A Real Story

I walked through our front door after work, expecting the usual evening routine—dinner, maybe some television, the comfortable predictability of newlywed life. Instead, my wife was sitting on our couch with a look I'd never seen before. Part excitement, part nervousness, maybe a little fear mixed in.

"We're going to have a baby," she said simply.

My first thought was excitement—pure, overwhelming joy. My second thought was panic. We were twenty years old. We'd been married exactly one month. We had planned to wait a few years, but God had other plans.

"We're not ready for this," I remember thinking. We barely knew how to take care of ourselves, let alone another human being. Our apartment was tiny, our bank account was smaller, and our experience with babies was practically nonexistent.

But looking back now, after raising six children, I can see God's perfect timing in ways I never could have imagined then. That first son became the steady older brother who helped welcome four more children into our family through foster care. His gentle heart was exactly what our family would need.

God knew what He was doing, even when we had no clue.

Biblical Reflection

When King David penned Psalm 127, he used two specific Hebrew concepts that change how we think about fatherhood. The word "gift" is mattanah, which refers to something given freely by someone in authority—not earned or deserved, but bestowed out of generosity. Your child isn't something you've achieved; they're something God has entrusted to your care.

The word "reward" is sakar, like wages paid for faithful service. But this isn't a paycheck you've earned for good behavior. It's more like a bonus given by a generous employer who sees potential in you that you might not see in yourself.

Here's what this means: God didn't make a mistake when He decided you should be this child's dad. He looked at your heart, your potential, and His ability to work through you, and He said, "This is exactly who I want for this job."

The weight you feel? That's appropriate. But the wonder you experience when you think about holding your child—that's God giving you a glimpse of how He feels about you. You are His child, and now He's inviting you into the sacred work of helping another person discover that same relationship.

Family Action Step

This week, create a simple ritual around Psalm 127:3. If your baby is already here, hold them while you read this verse aloud. If you're still waiting, place your hand on your wife's belly and speak these words over your unborn child.

Make this a daily practice for the next seven days. Just let the truth settle into your heart: this child is God's gift to you, and you are God's gift to them.

Reflection Questions

What specific fears about fatherhood feel most real to you right now, and how does viewing your child as God's gift change your perspective on those concerns?

When you think about being "chosen" by God to be this child's father, what does that stir up in your heart—gratitude, anxiety, excitement, or something else entirely?

Prayer & Blessing

Prayer for This Week

Father God, thank You for trusting me with this incredible responsibility. I confess that I feel unprepared and sometimes overwhelmed by what lies ahead. Help me to see this child through Your eyes—as a precious gift, not a burden. Give me wisdom for the decisions ahead, patience for sleepless nights, and faith to believe that You will equip me for every moment of this journey. I surrender my fears to You and ask for Your grace to be the father You've called me to be. Amen.

Father's Blessing to Speak Over Your Child

Little one, you are wanted, you are loved, and you are a gift from God Himself. May you grow strong in body and spirit, may you know your Heavenly Father's love through your earthly parents, and may you always remember that you were created for a purpose only you can fulfill. I pray God's protection over your life and His blessing on every step you take. In Jesus' name, amen.

WEEK 2

When You Feel Unprepared

"Instead, God chose things the world considers foolish in order to shame those who think they are wise."
— 1 Corinthians 1:27 (NLT)

A Real Story

The nurses were efficient and kind, but their medical jargon felt like a foreign language. Our son, barely weeks old, was inside a plastic tent filled with mist, and all I could do was watch while machines monitored his every breath. The diagnosis was croup, but to us twenty-year-olds, it might as well have been a death sentence.

I stood there feeling completely out of my league. Other fathers looked older, more composed, like they knew what questions to ask. I felt like a kid playing dress-up in grown-up clothes. Emergency room visits became our new normal—racing to the hospital at 2 AM, praying desperate prayers: "God, I don't know what I'm doing, but please help him breathe."

I remember thinking, "Somebody made a mistake here. I'm not qualified for this." But in those long nights of prayer and worry, God was building something in me—a dependence on Him that would become the foundation of everything that followed.

Years later, when we became foster parents to children with trauma and medical challenges, I realized those early hospital nights weren't just about our son getting well. They were about me learning that being unprepared by the world's standards doesn't disqualify you from being exactly who God needs you to be.

Biblical Reflection

Paul's words to the Corinthian church cut straight to the heart of every man who's ever felt inadequate. The Greek word for "foolish" is moros—from which we get "moron." Paul is saying God deliberately chooses people the world would consider completely unqualified.

Corinth prized intelligence, status, and achievement. Sound familiar? Our culture tells us good fathers need the right education, perfect income, ideal emotional intelligence, and years of experience.

God operates differently. He chooses shepherds to be kings, fishermen to be apostles, young men to be fathers of nations. He doesn't choose based on human qualifications because they can become sources of pride that interfere with dependence on Him.

When you feel unprepared, you're in excellent company. Moses, Gideon, and David all felt unprepared. The difference wasn't their natural ability—it was their willingness to let God work through their weaknesses.

Your sleepless nights, financial stress, and questions aren't disqualifications. They're invitations to depend on a God who specializes in extraordinary work through ordinary people who know they need Him.

Family Action Step

Write a brief letter to your child acknowledging your feelings of being unprepared, but expressing your commitment to trust God. Keep it simple: "I don't have all the answers, but I know the One who does, and I promise to seek His wisdom as I learn to be your dad."

Seal it and put it somewhere safe. You'll be amazed to look back and see how God used your honest uncertainty as the starting point for faithful fatherhood.

Reflection Questions

What specific area of fatherhood makes you feel most "unqualified," and how might God want to use that weakness to draw you closer to Him?

Looking at 1 Corinthians 1:27, what evidence do you see that God can work through your limitations rather than despite them?

Prayer & Blessing

Prayer for This Week

Lord, I come feeling small and unprepared. Your Word says You choose the unlikely and uncertain. Thank You for choosing me, not because I'm qualified, but because You are faithful. Use my weaknesses to display Your strength. When I'm uncertain, be my wisdom. When I'm afraid, be my courage. Help me lean into You. Amen.

Father's Blessing to Speak Over Your Child

Precious child, your daddy may not have all the answers, but he serves a God who does. May you grow knowing your worth comes from who you are, not what you achieve. May you see God's strength made perfect in weakness and remember He chooses ordinary people for extraordinary things. In Jesus' name, amen.

WEEK 3

Your Past Doesn't Define Your Future

"This means that anyone who belongs to Christ has become a new person. The old life is gone; a new life has begun!"
— 2 Corinthians 5:17 (NLT)

A Real Story

Looking down at my newborn son, I made a quiet promise: "You're going to have something I never had."

I grew up in a home where alcohol was the third parent—always present, always changing the rules. My parents weren't bad people, but they were broken, and their brokenness shaped our household. Dinner conversations were interrupted by arguments, promises forgotten, unpredictable swings between affection and anger.

By seventeen, I had two clear paths: follow the familiar pattern I'd watched my whole life, or choose something different. When I gave my life to Christ, it wasn't just about heaven someday—it was about breaking free from a legacy I didn't want to pass on.

Standing in that hospital room with my son, I felt the weight of that choice. This tiny person would never wonder if his father would be present, sober, and emotionally available. The cycle stopped here.

In Christ, I genuinely was a new person. The old patterns, the inherited brokenness—all of it was obsolete. God had given me something my parents never had: the power to choose differently.

Biblical Reflection

Paul's declaration wasn't theoretical—it was a practical truth for people trapped by their past. The Greek word "new" (kainos) doesn't just mean fresh, but completely different in quality, unprecedented. God doesn't just clean up your old life; He gives you an entirely different kind of life.

"Old life is gone" uses parerchomai—passed away completely, like a storm that leaves clear skies. Your father's anger, your family's broken promises—these influenced your past, but don't control your future.

Maybe you grew up with an absent, angry, or addicted father. Maybe you witnessed marriage patterns you don't want to repeat. The gospel says you're not doomed to repeat those mistakes because you're not living out of their resources anymore.

You can parent from God the Father's example—perfect love, infinite patience, unwavering faithfulness. Your painful experiences become tools God uses to help you parent with intentionality and compassion.

Family Action Step

Write down three things you experienced growing up that you want to be different for your child. Then write the opposite—the positive quality you want to bring because of Christ's work in your life.

Example: "I experienced unpredictability" becomes "I will provide stability."

Keep this list where you'll see it regularly. You're not parenting from your past; you're parenting from your new identity in Christ.

Reflection Questions

What specific fears do you have about repeating negative patterns, and how does being "a new person" in Christ speak to those concerns?

How might your difficult childhood experiences help you become a more intentional and compassionate father?

Prayer & Blessing

Prayer for This Week

Heavenly Father, thank You for breaking the chains of my past and making me new in Christ. Help me parent from Your example rather than broken patterns I inherited. Give me wisdom to recognize old habits and strength to choose Your way. Use even my painful experiences to make me a more compassionate father. Amen.

Father's Blessing to Speak Over Your Child

My precious child, you are part of a new story. The broken patterns of the past stop with me because Jesus has made our family new. You will grow up knowing consistent love and experiencing faithfulness that comes from a father who follows Christ. May you always know your worth and God's good plans for your life. In Jesus' name, amen.

WEEK 4

Trading Worry for Trust

"Look at the birds. They don't plant or harvest or store food in barns, for your heavenly Father feeds them. And aren't you far more valuable to him than they are?"
— Matthew 6:26 (NLT)

A Real Story

The social worker said she'd be with us for two weeks. Two weeks maximum, while they found a more permanent placement for this tiny two-year-old girl. We figured we could handle anything for two weeks.

That was twenty years ago. We still joke that it's been the longest two weeks of our lives.

When our son was four, we felt called to open our home to foster children. It seemed manageable—we had experience with one child and wanted to help. What we didn't anticipate was how quickly our family would grow. Within months, we discovered we were pregnant with our second child. Then the two-year-old's two half-sisters needed placement.

I have a photograph from the day all five children were in our house together for the first time. (Our sixth child came later.) The kids are laughing and smiling, but if you look at my wife and me in the background, we look like deer caught in headlights.

"What have we done?" I remember thinking. One child had felt challenging enough. Five felt impossible. The grocery bills, the laundry, the emotional needs of children who had experienced trauma—it all felt overwhelming. How do you feed five kids on a budget that was tight with one?

But somewhere in that chaos, we made a decision that changed everything. We decided to trade worry for trust. Instead of calculating whether we could handle this, we chose to believe that the God who had called us would provide everything we needed. And He has, for over two decades now.

Biblical Reflection

Jesus spoke to people who understood worry about provision—most lived day to day with no backup plans. The Greek word for "worry" (merimnao) means to be divided in mind, pulled in different directions by conflicting thoughts about potential problems.

For fathers, this worry feels almost responsible. Shouldn't we be concerned about college funds? Shouldn't we lose sleep over making the right decisions? Jesus isn't calling us to be careless—He's calling us to be dependent. Birds don't plan or store because they trust the One who feeds them daily.

Your Heavenly Father knows about the mortgage, medical bills, and college fund that isn't growing fast enough. He knows your child's personality, future struggles, and need for wisdom you don't yet possess. You are far more valuable to Him than the birds He faithfully feeds every day.

This doesn't mean you shouldn't plan or work hard. It means you don't have to carry the crushing weight of being your family's ultimate provider. That job belongs to Someone with infinitely greater resources and perfect wisdom.

Family Action Step

Start a "God's Provision Journal" this week. Each day, write down one way you saw God provide—financial, emotional, physical, or spiritual. Include small things like finding what you needed on sale or having a peaceful moment when you needed it most.

At week's end, read through the list together. Let it build your faith and train your eyes to see God's faithful care in everyday moments.

Reflection Questions

What specific worries about providing for your family consume the most energy, and how might God be inviting you to trust Him more in those areas?

Looking back, what are examples of God's provision that you might have missed at the time but can see now?

Prayer & Blessing

Prayer for This Week

Father, You know the weight I carry about providing for my family. I confess that I often try to carry burdens that belong to You alone. Help me trust Your provision the way birds trust You to feed them each day. Give me wisdom to be responsible without being anxious. Thank You for caring for my family even more than I do. Amen.

Father's Blessing to Speak Over Your Child

Beloved child, your Heavenly Father knows every need you'll ever have. May you grow up trusting His faithful provision, knowing you are precious beyond measure. May you bring your worries to Him rather than carry them alone, remembering you are far more valuable than the birds He feeds each day. In Jesus' name, amen.

Growing Your Faith:

Building spiritual habits that stick

WEEK 5

Prayer That Works

"Don't worry about anything; instead, pray about everything. Tell God what you need, and thank him for all he has done."
— Philippians 4:6-7 (NLT)

A Real Story

The cupboards were empty, and so was our bank account. We stood in our kitchen, opening and closing cabinet doors as if food might magically appear. Our son had no idea his parents were calculating how many days we could stretch what little we had left.

We were young, proud, and hesitant to ask for help. So instead of swallowing our pride, we prayed: "God, we need help. Our son needs dinner, and we don't know what to do. Please provide."

Twenty minutes later, there was a knock at our door. Our neighbor stood on our front step with an apologetic smile. "I hope this isn't weird, but we just bought a new freezer, and it came with more meat than we have room for. I was wondering if you could use some of it?"

Some people would call it a coincidence. But we knew exactly what it was: God answering the prayer of two young parents who had nowhere else to turn. That evening, I learned something about prayer that changed everything. Prayer isn't about convincing God to care—He already cares more than we do. Prayer is about bringing our needs to Someone who has the power to meet them.

Biblical Reflection

Paul wrote these words from a Roman prison cell, which gives them weight. This wasn't theory; this was someone who had tested God's faithfulness in challenging circumstances and found it reliable.

"Don't worry about anything" in Greek is meden merimna—literally "not even one thing." Paul isn't being hyperbolic; he's being comprehensive. Your child's health, job security, finances, parenting decisions—nothing is too big for God or too small for Him to care about.

The word "pray" (proseuchomai) specifically means bringing requests to God. This isn't meditation; it's asking for help from Someone who can provide it. Paul balances this with thanksgiving, acknowledging what God has already done while asking for what we still need.

For fathers, this creates a powerful framework. When your baby won't sleep, when bills pile up, when you're unsure about decisions—these become opportunities for prayer rather than reasons for panic.

Family Action Step

Establish a "Prayer Before Panic" practice this week. When you feel worry rising about any aspect of fatherhood, stop and pray immediately before anxiety builds.

Keep it simple: "God, I'm worried about ______. I need Your help. Thank You that You care about our family's needs even more than I do." Then thank Him for one specific way He's already provided.

Do this consistently for seven days and notice how it changes your stress level and awareness of God's care.

Reflection Questions

What specific worries about providing for or protecting your family keep you awake at night, and how might bringing these directly to God change your perspective?

Can you think of a time when God provided for your family in a way that seemed like more than a coincidence? How does that strengthen your faith for current concerns?

Prayer & Blessing

Prayer for This Week

Lord, I confess that I often try to carry my family's security on my shoulders. Forgive my pride in being reluctant to ask for help, and the fear that makes me doubt Your provision. Teach me to bring every concern to You before it becomes overwhelming worry. Help me model trust for my children rather than anxiety. Amen.

Father's Blessing

Precious one, you serve a God who knows every need before you ask and cares about every detail of your life. May you grow up knowing that worry is never your portion because your Heavenly Father is always your provider. May you bring your concerns to Him with confidence, trusting His timing and resting in His care. In Jesus' name, amen.

WEEK 6

Finding Time in the Word

"Your word is a lamp to guide my feet and a light for my path."
— Psalm 119:105 (NLT)

A Real Story

By the time evening came, I was completely spent. Work, helping with the baby, household chores—all I wanted was to collapse on the couch and watch whatever game was on television.

The Bible on my nightstand felt like another burden. I knew I should be reading it, especially as a new father needing God's wisdom. But every time I tried, the words blurred together. After fighting to keep my eyes open for five minutes, I'd give up, feeling like another failure.

My Christian friends didn't help: "You need to be in the Word daily, especially now that you're a father." They talked about hour-long quiet times as if I had unlimited energy and free time.

Everything changed when I stopped trying to be the perfect Bible student and started being an honest one. Instead of attempting entire chapters while exhausted, I began reading just two or three verses. Sometimes during lunch at work, sometimes on my phone while holding a napping baby.

Those small doses of Scripture began sustaining me in ways I hadn't expected. A verse about God's strength in weakness would come to mind during tough days. A promise about faithfulness would encourage me during 2 AM feedings.

I discovered that God's Word isn't just information to study—it's nourishment for the soul, and even small portions provide exactly what you need for the next step.

Biblical Reflection

The psalmist's lamp metaphor is perfect for busy fathers. Ancient oil lamps provided just enough light for the immediate step ahead—not a floodlight for the whole journey, but focused light for the path directly in front of you.

The Hebrew word for "lamp" (ner) refers to something small, portable, and practical. This isn't about mastering theology; it's about getting enough light to see the next step—wisdom for today's decisions, strength for today's challenges.

Scripture meets us where we are, not where we think we should be. When you're running on empty, one verse about God's faithfulness can carry more weight than an entire chapter might in a different season. God honors the two minutes you have available just as much as the hour you don't.

Different seasons call for different approaches. The goal isn't impressing God with discipline, but staying connected to the source of wisdom and strength you desperately need as a father.

Family Action Step

Implement the "Three Verse Rule" this week. Read just three verses each day at a time that actually works—lunch break, coffee time, before bed.

Write down one thing that stood out from those verses. Don't aim for profound insights; just note something relevant to your day or fatherhood.

Review your notes at week's end. You'll be surprised how much God speaks through small portions of His Word.

Reflection Questions

What obstacles make Bible reading difficult since becoming a father, and how might adjusting expectations help your spiritual growth?

Can you recall a specific verse that gave you strength during a challenging parenting moment? How did that show you Scripture's practical power?

Prayer & Blessing

Prayer for This Week

Lord, forgive me for treating Your Word like another burden instead of the strength it provides. Help me approach You with my limited time and energy, knowing You value honest availability over impressive spirituality. Meet me in small moments and speak through brief encounters with Scripture. Give me today's wisdom, strength, and peace. Amen.

Father's Blessing to Speak Over Your Child

Dear child, may you grow up seeing God's Word treasured as a gift, not a burden. May you learn from your father's example to turn to Scripture for guidance. May God's truth light your path through every season, providing exactly what you need for whatever lies ahead. In Jesus' name, amen.

WEEK 7

When You Need Wisdom Fast

"If you need wisdom, ask our generous God, and he will give it to you. He will not rebuke you for asking."
— James 1:5 (NLT)

A Real Story

Our two-year-old foster daughter—the one who was supposed to be with us for just two weeks—was having one of those epic meltdowns that make you question every parenting decision you've ever made. She was throwing herself on the floor, screaming about something that seemed completely unreasonable, and I found myself standing there with no clue how to respond.

This wasn't typical toddler behavior. This was a child who had experienced trauma, and her meltdowns were intense and heartbreaking. My first instinct was to try reasoning with her, but that only seemed to escalate things. Traditional timeout methods felt wrong for a child who had already experienced too much isolation.

Then something came to mind—not a verse this time, but a principle I'd absorbed from reading about God's character: sometimes the best response to chaos is joy. Instead of matching her intensity with correction, we gently placed her in her room for safety and cranked up the music in the living room. Dance party time with the other kids.

The transformation was remarkable. Within minutes, her screaming turned to curious silence as she heard laughter and music. Eventually, the fear of missing out won, and she emerged from her room, tears still on her cheeks but ready to join the celebration.

That approach became our go-to strategy for her meltdowns. The more I read Scripture and learned about God's patient, creative love, the more I found unconventional but effective ways to parent children who needed healing along with discipline. God's wisdom often looked different from what I expected, but it always worked better than my natural responses.

Biblical Reflection

James wrote to believers facing difficult decisions who needed real answers right now. The Greek word for "wisdom" (sophia) isn't just knowledge—it's the ability to make good decisions under pressure.

What makes this promise remarkable is its simplicity. James doesn't require fasting, counselling sessions, or complex processes. He says ask. Just bring your needs directly to God. For fathers facing split-second parenting decisions, you can access divine wisdom instantly through simple prayer.

God gives wisdom generously and without criticism. He won't make you feel foolish for needing help. He understands that parenting requires wisdom you don't naturally possess.

Here's the key: wisdom often comes through Scripture you've already read. God brings relevant truth to mind from what you've learned. This is why consistent Bible reading matters—you're building a foundation of biblical wisdom that God can draw from when you need it most.

Family Action Step

This week, practice "instant wisdom prayers" in parenting moments. When you face a decision about discipline, patience, or how to respond to your child's behavior, pause for just three seconds and pray: "God, I need wisdom right now."

Don't wait for dramatic revelations. Look for gentle promptings, relevant verses that come to mind, or simply a sense of peace about which direction to take. Keep a mental note of how God provides guidance in these quick moments.

Reflection Questions

Can you think of a recent parenting situation where you wished you had more wisdom in the moment? How might asking God directly for guidance have changed your response?

What connection do you see between regular Bible reading (even small amounts) and having God's wisdom available when you need it quickly?

Prayer & Blessing

Prayer for This Week

Father, thank You for promising to give wisdom generously to anyone who asks. I confess that I often rely on my own understanding instead of turning to You in parenting moments. Help me to develop the habit of asking for Your guidance quickly and confidently. Fill my mind with biblical truth that You can bring to my remembrance when I need it most. Make me quick to seek Your wisdom and quick to trust it. Amen.

Father's Blessing to Speak Over Your Child

Precious child, may you grow up seeing your father seek God's wisdom in both big and small decisions. May you learn that God's guidance is always available to those who ask, and may you develop the habit of turning to Him for wisdom throughout your life. May His truth guide your steps and His wisdom shape your choices. In Jesus' name, amen.

WEEK 8

Staying Connected to Your Church Family

"And let us not neglect our meeting together,
as some people do, but encourage one another,
especially now that the day of his return is drawing near."
— Hebrews 10:25 (NLT)

A Real Story

It was supposed to be a fresh start. After some disagreements at our home church, we decided to try somewhere new. The drive was longer, but we figured it might be good to have a clean slate, especially with our growing family and the challenges that come with foster care.

Those six months felt like the longest six months of our lives. Sunday mornings became exercises in isolation. We'd sit in the back row, smile politely during the greeting time, and leave immediately after the service. No one knew our story, our struggles, or our kids' unique needs. When our foster daughter had particularly difficult weeks, there was no one to call for prayer or support. When we celebrated small victories, we celebrated alone.

Then one evening, our former pastor showed up on our front porch. He didn't come to lecture us about leaving—he came to tell us we were missed and to invite us home. "Your church family wants you back," he said simply.

We didn't hesitate. The next Sunday, we walked back into our home church, and it felt like exhaling after holding our breath for six months. People who knew our children's names welcomed them with genuine excitement. Families who understood our unique challenges offered help and support. We were reminded that church isn't just about attending services—it's about belonging to a family that walks through life together.

Biblical Reflection

The writer of Hebrews understood something crucial about human nature: we naturally drift toward isolation, especially when life gets complicated. The Greek word for "neglect" (egkataleipo) means to abandon or forsake completely. It's not just missing a few Sundays—it's the gradual disconnection that happens when we convince ourselves we can handle life alone.

For new fathers, this tendency toward isolation can feel almost necessary. Sunday mornings are harder with babies. Church activities conflict with nap schedules. The energy required to maintain relationships feels overwhelming when you're already stretched thin.

But the writer of Hebrews argues that the Christian community becomes more important, not less, during challenging seasons. The word "encourage" (parakaleo) literally means to call alongside—it's the picture of someone walking next to you through difficult terrain, offering strength and perspective you can't provide for yourself.

As fathers, we need other dads who understand the unique pressures we face. We need families who can share practical wisdom about parenting challenges. We need a church community that knows our children's names, prays for our struggles, and celebrates our victories.

Family Action Step

This week, take one concrete step to strengthen your connection to your church family. If you've been disconnected, reach out to someone you miss. If you're regularly attending but not really connecting, introduce yourself to one new family or couple.

Reflection Questions

What factors (schedule, energy, past hurts) have made it difficult to maintain strong connections with your church family since becoming a father, and how might you address one of those obstacles?

How do you want your children to view church community, and what steps can you take now to model healthy engagement with your faith family?

Prayer & Blessing

Prayer for This Week

Father, thank You for promising to give wisdom generously to anyone who asks. I confess that I often rely on my own understanding instead of turning to You in parenting moments. Help me to develop the habit of asking for Your guidance quickly and confidently. Fill my mind with biblical truth that You can bring to my remembrance when I need it most. Make me quick to seek Your wisdom and quick to trust it. Amen.

Father's Blessing to Speak Over Your Child

Precious child, may you grow up seeing your father seek God's wisdom in both big and small decisions. May you learn that God's guidance is always available to those who ask, and may you develop the habit of turning to Him for wisdom throughout your life. May His truth guide your steps and His wisdom shape your choices. In Jesus' name, amen.

Building Character:

Becoming the man your family needs

WEEK 9

Patience When You're Running on Empty

"But the Holy Spirit produces this kind of fruit in our lives: love, joy, peace, patience, kindness, goodness, faithfulness, gentleness, and self-control. There is no law against these things!"
— Galatians 5:22-23 (NLT)

A Real Story

It was 6:47 AM on the first day of school, and chaos had already claimed victory over our household.

The baby had been up since 4 AM with another ear infection. My wife was juggling pump parts and coffee while getting ready for work. Our toddler had discovered that maple syrup makes excellent finger paint, and our three school-aged kids were in various states of meltdown over missing backpacks, forgotten homework, and having "nothing to wear."

"Dad, I can't find my math folder!" came from upstairs. "Daddy, I'm hungry, but I don't want breakfast!" came from the kitchen. "WAAAAAHHH!" came from everywhere, courtesy of our overtired baby.

I felt it rising—that familiar cocktail of frustration and exhaustion. My jaw clenched. My voice got sharp. "Just... everybody just STOP for a second!" The house went silent. Five pairs of eyes stared at me, and I saw what I'd become—the impatient father I swore I'd never be. My oldest looked genuinely hurt, and I realized my empty tank had just contaminated the entire morning.

That's when it hit me: I can't give what I don't have. But maybe, just maybe, God could give what I don't have.

Biblical Reflection

Paul lists patience as one of the fruits of the Spirit, and there's something profound about its placement in that list. It comes right after peace, as if to say that true patience flows from an inner calm that only comes from God. The Greek word here is makrothymia—literally "long-tempered" as opposed to short-tempered. It's the supernatural capacity to remain steady and kind under pressure, especially when dealing with people who are testing your limits.

As fathers, we face unique patience challenges. We're trying to teach life lessons to children who don't want to learn them and maintain our cool when everything feels out of control. But this kind of patience isn't something we muster up through willpower—it's fruit that the Holy Spirit produces in our lives. When we're running on empty, we can tap into a divine source of patience that doesn't depend on how much sleep we got or how well-behaved our kids are.

Family Action Step

This week, develop a three-second prayer for patience moments. When you feel your frustration rising—whether it's during a meltdown, bedtime resistance, or daily chaos—take three seconds to silently pray: "Holy Spirit, give me Your patience right now."

Practice this when the stakes are low, so it becomes natural when tensions are high. Also, identify your patience danger zones. Are you more likely to lose it when you're hungry, tired, or rushing? Build small buffers into those situations when possible, and give yourself grace when you fall short.

Reflection Questions

When do you most struggle with patience as a father, and what does that reveal about your need for God's strength in parenting?

How might your children's understanding of God's patience with them be shaped by experiencing your patience with them, both when you succeed and when you fail and ask forgiveness?

Prayer & Blessing

Prayer for This Week

Father, I confess that I often try to parent in my own strength, and my patience runs out quickly. Thank You for Your patience with me, never runs dry, even when I'm demanding, rebellious, or unreasonable. Holy Spirit, produce supernatural patience in my life. Help me to respond to my children's needs and behaviors from Your abundance, not from my empty reserves. When I fail, give me the humility to apologize and model what it looks like to receive Your forgiveness. Make me the kind of father who points my children to Your endless patience with them. Amen.

Father's Blessing to Speak Over Your Child

Dear child, may you experience God's perfect patience through your imperfect father. When I am short-tempered, may you still understand that your Heavenly Father's patience with you never runs out. May you grow in patience with others as you experience patience from God. And may you always know that your worth is not determined by your behavior, but by God's unchanging love for you. In Jesus' name, amen.

WEEK 10

Leading by Serving

"But among you it will be different. Whoever wants to be a leader among you must be your servant. And whoever wants to be first among you must be the slave of everyone else."
— Mark 10:43-44 (NLT)

A Real Story

Years later, my kids don't remember most of my parenting lectures or my attempts at profound teachable moments. But they still talk about story time.

Every night for what felt like forever, I'd settle into the rocking chair with whoever wanted to listen, and we'd journey to Narnia together. I gave Aslan a deep, regal voice that made the room feel sacred. Mr. Tumnus got a nervous, stuttering delivery. The White Witch was appropriately menacing, and Edmund's voice cracked with guilt and redemption.

I'm sure my Reep cheep voice changed over the months—sometimes squeaky, sometimes more dignified—but my kids never called me out on it. They were too caught up in the magic I was trying to create for them.

Looking back, those weren't just bedtime stories. They were acts of service. I could have handed them the books and told them to read independently. I could have played an audiobook. Instead, I chose to give them something that required my presence, my energy, and my willingness to sound ridiculous for their sake.

Now, when they think of leadership—when they think of what it means to be a father—they don't picture someone barking orders or demanding respect. They picture someone who cared enough to do voices, night after night, because it mattered to them.

Biblical Reflection

Jesus completely redefined leadership. In a culture where leaders demanded service from others, He served others. Where leaders sought the highest positions, He took the lowest. Where leaders expected to be waited on, He washed feet.

As fathers, we often think leadership means being the decision-maker, the authority figure, the one who's in charge. And there's truth to that—we do have responsibility and authority in our homes. But Jesus shows us that true leadership is measured not by how many people serve us, but by how many people we serve.

This servant leadership looks different in every family. It might be reading bedtime stories with silly voices. It might be learning your daughter's favorite songs so you can sing along in the car. It might be showing up to every game, every recital, every ordinary Tuesday that matters to your child.

When we lead by serving, we earn a different kind of respect—not the fear-based compliance that comes from power, but the genuine honor that comes from love. Our children learn that strength is used to lift others up, not to push them down.

Family Action Step

This week, choose one way to serve your family that requires your personal investment—something that only you can do, not something that can be delegated or automated. It might be learning a new skill your child is interested in, creating a special tradition, or simply being fully present during an activity that matters to them.

The goal isn't to add another task to your list, but to find opportunities where your leadership looks like love in action.

Reflection Questions

What are some ways you currently serve your family that your children might remember years from now, and how do these acts of service demonstrate godly leadership?

How can you model for your children that true strength is found in serving others, not in being served by them?

Prayer & Blessing

Prayer for This Week

Jesus, thank You for showing me that leadership begins with service. Help me to lead my family not through demands or position, but through love that gets down on the floor, reads the stories, and enters into their world. Give me eyes to see the small ways I can serve my children today, knowing that these moments are building their understanding of what godly leadership looks like. Make me a father who earns respect through sacrifice, not demands it through authority. Amen.

Father's Blessing to Speak Over Your Child

Dear child, may you grow up understanding that true leaders are servants, and that real strength is found in lifting others. May you see in your father a man who uses his authority to serve, protect, and love his family. And may you carry this heart of servant leadership into every relationship and responsibility God gives you. In Jesus' name, amen.

WEEK 11

Quick to Listen, Slow to Anger

"Understand this, my dear brothers and sisters: You must all be quick to listen, slow to speak, and slow to get angry. Human anger does not produce the righteousness that God desires."
— James 1:19-20 (NLT)

A Real Story

I used to be the guy who had an opinion about everything and wasn't shy about sharing it. Quick with a comeback, faster with frustration, and always ready to make my point heard. It worked, or at least I thought it did.

Then I became a father.

The first time my toddler threw a full-scale meltdown in the grocery store, my instinct was to match his energy. Louder voice, sharper words, immediate consequences. But instead of resolving the situation, I escalated it. My son cried harder, other parents stared, and I realized that the approach that had gotten me through debates as a single man was destroying my relationship with my child.

The wake-up call came when my wife gently said, "He's not your opponent. He's your son." She was right. I'd been treating parenting like a battle to be won instead of a relationship to be nurtured. Learning to be slow to anger meant taking deep breaths, asking "What is my child really trying to tell me?" and choosing curiosity over immediate correction.

Biblical Reflection

James gives us a powerful formula for healthy relationships: quick to listen, slow to speak, slow to anger. Notice the order—listening comes first, speaking comes second, and anger should be the last resort, not the first response.

As fathers, we carry a lot of pressure, and when we're overwhelmed, our default mode often becomes quick to speak and quick to anger. But James reminds us that human anger doesn't produce the righteousness God desires or create the kind of home where children feel safe to be honest and grow.

Being quick to listen means genuinely trying to understand what's behind our children's behavior. Being slow to speak gives us time to respond thoughtfully. And being slow to anger creates space for wisdom instead of escalation. This doesn't mean we become passive—it means we lead our families from strength and self-control rather than from our overflow of frustration.

Family Action Step

This week, practice the "pause and listen" approach when you feel your frustration rising with your children. Before responding to challenging behavior, take three deep breaths and ask yourself: "What is my child really trying to communicate?"

Try listening for the need behind the behavior before jumping to correction. Sometimes a child who's "being difficult" is actually tired, overwhelmed, or feeling disconnected from you.

Keep a mental note of moments when you successfully chose to listen first. Notice how it changes both your response and your child's reaction.

Reflection Questions

What triggers your quick anger as a father, and how might those triggers be connected to your own stress or overwhelm rather than your children's behavior?

How do you want your children to remember your voice and your presence during their difficult moments—and what steps can you take to create those memories?

Prayer & Blessing

Prayer for This Week

Father, forgive me for the times I've let my frustration and overwhelm spill onto my family. Help me to be quick to listen to my children's hearts, not just their words. Give me patience to understand what's really going on before I react. Make me slow to speak harsh words and slow to let anger control my responses. When I'm feeling overwhelmed, remind me that my family needs my strength and wisdom, not my stress and frustration. Help me create a home where grace is louder than my anger. Amen.

Father's Blessing to Speak Over Your Child

Dear child, may you always feel heard and understood in our home. When you're struggling, may you find in your father someone who listens first and loves you through your hardest moments. May you learn from my example that strength means controlling your anger, not letting it control you. And may you always know that no behavior could ever change how much you are loved. In Jesus' name, amen.

WEEK 12

Grace for Your Mistakes

"But if we confess our sins to him, he is faithful and just to forgive us our sins and to cleanse us from all wickedness."
— 1 John 1:9 (NLT)

A Real Story

I'm not even sure I'm ready to write down how badly I messed up that day. The details still make me cringe with shame—the harsh words, the lost temper, the way I let my stress and frustration explode all over the people I love most.

What I can tell you is this: I hurt my family. Not just their feelings, but their trust in me as the man who's supposed to protect and lead them with love. I saw it in their eyes—confusion, disappointment, and something that looked dangerously close to fear.

That night, after the house was quiet and I'd had time to face what I'd done, I knew there was only one path forward. Not excuses, not justification, not waiting for it to blow over. I had to own it completely.

So I gathered my family together the next day. I looked my children in the eyes and said the hardest words I'd ever spoken as a father: "I was wrong. I hurt you. I'm sorry. Will you forgive me?"

The grace that followed wasn't immediate or easy, but it was real. My children saw their father as a man who could admit his failures and ask for forgiveness. They learned that even dads make mistakes, but that real men take responsibility for them.

Biblical Reflection

John's promise of forgiveness is radical: when we confess our sins, God doesn't just overlook them—He cleanses us completely. As fathers, we need this truth desperately because we will mess up. Not if, but when.

The temptation after we fail our families is either to minimize our mistakes or to wallow in guilt. But confession offers a third way—honest acknowledgment followed by genuine forgiveness. When we model this with our children, we teach them that mistakes don't define us, but how we handle them does.

Asking our children for forgiveness doesn't undermine our authority—it strengthens it. It shows them what godly leadership actually looks like: humble, accountable, and secure enough to admit wrongs. Our children learn that their father is human, that God's grace covers even parenting failures, and that relationships can be restored after they've been damaged.

Family Action Step

If you've hurt your family recently through anger, harshness, or neglect, don't wait for the perfect moment to address it. Sit down with those you've wronged—whether it's your spouse, your children, or both—and offer a genuine apology without excuses or conditions.

If you can't think of recent failures, ask God to show you blind spots where you might need to seek forgiveness. Sometimes we're the last to see our own mistakes.

Remember: confession to God is essential, but when we've hurt our families, confession to them is also necessary for healing and restoration.

Reflection Questions

What prevents you from admitting mistakes to your children—pride, fear of losing respect, or something else—and how might your willingness to seek forgiveness actually strengthen your relationship with them?

How do you want your children to handle their own failures and mistakes, and what are you modelling for them through your own response to sin and forgiveness?

Prayer & Blessing

Prayer for This Week

Father, I confess that I am a flawed and imperfect dad who needs Your grace every day. Thank You that Your forgiveness is complete and Your love for me doesn't depend on my perfect parenting. Give me the humility to admit when I'm wrong and the courage to seek forgiveness from those I've hurt. Help my children see that our family is built on grace, not perfection, and that real strength is found in admitting our need for You. Restore what I've broken and use even my failures to point my family to Your perfect love. Amen.

Father's Blessing to Speak Over Your Child

Dear child, may you grow up in a home where grace is greater than our mistakes and forgiveness is always available. When your father fails you, may you see God's heart in his willingness to admit wrong and ask forgiveness. May you learn that being human means needing grace, and that God's love for our family is bigger than any mistake we could ever make. In Jesus' name, amen.

Loving Your Wife Well:

Strengthening your Marriage through this Transition

WEEK 13

Love in Action

Theme Verse: "For husbands, this means love your wives, just as Christ loved the church. He gave up his life for her." — Ephesians 5:25 (NLT)

A Real Story

We were blessed to live near my wife's parents during those early years of raising kids. They were gracious beyond measure, always willing to take the children for a few hours so we could have our weekly date night.

Most couples might have used that time for fancy restaurants or movie dates. Not us. We were too exhausted for elaborate plans and too broke for expensive outings. More often than not, our "date night" meant driving home to an empty house, ordering takeout, and sitting together on the porch swing in our backyard.

We'd sit there in comfortable silence, sometimes talking about dreams for our family, sometimes just listening to the crickets. No crying babies, no demanding voices, no sticky fingers pulling at our clothes. Just us, remembering why we fell in love in the first place.

Those simple evenings on the porch swing became sacred to us. It wasn't about the grand gestures or romantic destinations. It was about choosing to prioritize our relationship even when we had nothing left to give except our presence. It was love in action during the most depleting season of our lives.

Years later, my wife still talks about those quiet moments together. They reminded us both that our marriage was worth protecting, even when—especially when—everything else felt overwhelming.

Biblical Reflection

Paul's command to love our wives as Christ loved the church sets an impossibly high standard. Christ's love was sacrificial, selfless, and constant. As new fathers, we often feel like we barely have enough energy left for ourselves, much less sacrificial love for our wives.

But notice that Paul doesn't say "when you feel like it" or "when circumstances are ideal." Love in action means choosing to serve our wives, especially when we're both running on empty. It means recognizing that she's carrying the same exhaustion, the same overwhelm, the same depletion that we are.

Sometimes love looks like planning elaborate surprises. But more often, especially in the early parenting years, love looks like small, consistent choices: protecting time together, sharing the mental load of family life, and choosing to see her as your partner, not just the mother of your children.

When we prioritize our marriage during these demanding years, we're not just loving our wives—we're creating the stable foundation our children need. They're watching us model what committed love looks like when life gets hard.

Family Action Step

This week, identify one small but consistent way to show love to your wife that doesn't require extra money or elaborate planning. It might be protecting a weekly connection time (even if it's just fifteen minutes), taking over bedtime routine one night a week, or simply asking "How can I help you today?" and actually following through.

The goal isn't grand gestures—it's consistent choices that communicate "You matter to me" even when life feels overwhelming. Look for ways to serve her that acknowledge the specific challenges she's facing as a new mom.

Reflection Questions

How has becoming a father changed your ability to love your wife well, and what adjustments do you need to make to prioritize your marriage during this season?

What would your wife say she needs most from you right now, and how can you provide that even when you're both exhausted?

Prayer & Blessing

Prayer for This Week

Lord, help me to love my wife with the same sacrificial love You showed the church. In this exhausting season of new parenthood, give me eyes to see her needs and strength to serve her even when I'm depleted. Remind me that our marriage is the foundation of our family, and that loving her well is one of the greatest gifts I can give our children. Show me practical ways to demonstrate my love through actions, not just words. Amen.

Father's Blessing to Speak Over Your Child

Dear child, may you grow up seeing your father love your mother with consistent, sacrificial care. May you witness a marriage built on service, respect, and genuine partnership. And may this example shape your understanding of what real love looks like—not just in feelings, but in daily choices to put another person's needs before your own. In Jesus' name, amen.

WEEK 14

Really Hearing Her

Theme Verse: "Spouting off before listening to the facts is both shameful and foolish."
— Proverbs 18:13 (NLT)

A Real Story

She was telling me about her day—how overwhelming it felt to manage the baby's feeding schedule while keeping up with household tasks, how isolated she sometimes felt during those long afternoons, how she wondered if she was doing anything right as a new mom.

My brain immediately went into fix-it mode. "Well, maybe you could try scheduling the baby's naps differently," I offered. "Or we could hire someone to help with cleaning. And you should definitely get out more—maybe join that mom's group at church."

The look on her face stopped me cold. It wasn't gratitude for my brilliant solutions. It was frustration, maybe even hurt.

"I don't need you to fix it," she said quietly. "I just need you to hear me."

That's when it hit me: I hadn't been listening to understand—I'd been listening to solve. While she was sharing her heart about the emotional weight of new motherhood, I was already three steps ahead, mentally organizing action plans and practical solutions.

She didn't need a consultant. She needed her husband. She needed someone who could sit with her in the difficult feelings without immediately trying to make them go away. Sometimes the most loving thing I could do was simply say, "That sounds really hard. Tell me more."

Biblical Reflection

Solomon warns us about the foolishness of responding before we've truly listened. As men, we're often wired to solve problems quickly, but this instinct can actually damage our relationships when what's needed isn't solutions but understanding.

When our wives share their struggles with us, they're usually not asking us to fix their circumstances—they're inviting us into their experience. The exhaustion, the uncertainty, the overwhelming nature of new motherhood—these aren't just problems to be solved. They're feelings to be acknowledged and burdens to be shared.

Real listening means putting aside our need to have answers and choosing instead to have presence. It means asking follow-up questions, validating emotions, and resisting the urge to jump immediately into problem-solving mode. Sometimes the most powerful thing we can say is "I hear you" instead of "Here's what you should do."

When we listen well, we communicate that our wives' inner lives matter to us, not just their productivity or happiness. We show them that their feelings are valid and important, even when we can't immediately make everything better.

Family Action Step

This week, practice listening to your wife without offering solutions unless she specifically asks for them. When she shares something difficult, try responding with phrases like "That sounds overwhelming" or "Tell me more about that" before jumping to advice.

Pay attention to the difference between conversations where she's venting versus conversations where she's actually asking for your input. Often, she'll tell you which one it is if you listen carefully to how she frames the conversation.

Set aside the phone and other distractions when she's talking to you. Give her your full attention and resist the urge to multitask while she's sharing her heart.

Reflection Questions

What prevents you from listening fully to your wife—the urge to fix, discomfort with emotions, or distraction—and how can you create space for better connection?

How might your wife's experience of new motherhood be different from your experience of new fatherhood, and what does she most need from you during this season?

Prayer & Blessing

Prayer for This Week

Father, teach me to listen to my wife with the same patience and attention that You listen to me. Help me resist the urge to fix everything and instead learn to be present with her in both joy and struggle. Give me wisdom to know when she needs solutions and when she simply needs to be heard. Make me the kind of husband who creates a safe space for her to share her heart without judgment or immediate advice. Show me how to love her by truly understanding her experience. Amen.

Father's Blessing to Speak Over Your Child

Dear child, may you learn from watching your parents that real love includes deep listening and genuine understanding. May you see your father honor your mother by giving her his full attention and validating her experiences. And may you grow up knowing that your own voice matters and that you have parents who will always listen to your heart. In Jesus' name, amen.

WEEK 15

Teamwork Through the Tough Times

"A person standing alone can be attacked and defeated, but two can stand back-to-back and conquer. Three are even better, for a triple-braided cord is not easily broken."
— Ecclesiastes 4:12 (NLT)

A Real Story

Spring baseball season used to make me break out in a cold sweat. All five of our kids played (remember the sixth one came later), often on different teams with overlapping schedules. Tuesday night: three games at three different fields. Saturday morning: double-headers that started at the same time on opposite sides of town.

At first, my wife and I tried to handle it separately. I'd take two kids to their games, she'd take the other two to theirs. We'd text updates, feel guilty about missing each other's games, and come home exhausted and disconnected. The kids started keeping score of who had more parental support in the stands.

That's when we realized we were attacking this challenge all wrong. Instead of dividing and conquering, we needed to work as a unified team with a clear strategy.

We sat down with a calendar and color-coded every game. We identified which games were most important to each child and made sure at least one parent was at those. For conflicts, we coordinated with other parents for carpooling. In some games, one kid would ride with a friend's family so we could focus on a sibling's championship game.

The magic happened when we started communicating our plan to the kids. "Dad's going to Tommy's playoff game, but Mom will be at your scrimmage. Next week, we'll both be at your tournament." Suddenly, they weren't competing for our attention—they were part of the team effort to make it all work.

Biblical Reflection

Solomon understood something crucial about facing life's challenges: we're stronger together than apart. The image of a triple-braided cord speaks to the power of unity—when individual strengths are woven together, they create something much more resilient than the sum of their parts.

As parents, we often default to divide-and-conquer strategies when life gets overwhelming. But this can leave us feeling isolated, competing instead of collaborating, and ultimately weakened by the very challenges we're trying to manage.

True teamwork in marriage means more than just splitting duties—it means facing challenges with a unified strategy, shared values, and mutual support. When we work together instead of separately, we model for our children what partnership looks like under pressure.

The "third cord" in our family's braid is often God's wisdom guiding our decisions, other families who support us, or simply the strength that comes when we stop trying to handle everything on our own.

Family Action Step

This week, identify one area where you and your wife are handling challenges separately that might be better approached as a team. It could be managing kids' schedules, household responsibilities, or even parenting decisions.

Sit down together and create a unified strategy. Instead of "you handle this, I'll handle that," ask, "how can we handle this together?" Look for ways to support each other rather than just dividing the load.

Communicate your team approach to your children so they understand you're working together, not against each other or in competition for their loyalty.

Reflection Questions

Where in your family life are you and your wife working separately when you could be working together, and what would need to change to make that happen?

How do your children see you and your wife handling challenges, as a unified team or as individuals managing separate responsibilities, and what does that teach them about partnership?

Prayer & Blessing

Prayer for This Week

Father, thank You for the gift of partnership in marriage and family life. Help my wife and me face challenges as a unified team rather than trying to handle everything separately. Give us wisdom to know when to divide responsibilities and when to stand together. Show us how to support each other's strengths and cover each other's weaknesses. Make our family a place where teamwork is stronger than individual effort, and where Your presence is the cord that holds us all together. Amen.

Father's Blessing to Speak Over Your Child

Dear child, may you grow up seeing your parents work as a team through every challenge life brings. May you learn that true strength comes not from going it alone, but from standing together with people who love you. And may you always know that our family faces everything together, with God as our foundation and each other as our support. In Jesus' name, amen.

WEEK 16

Keeping Romance Alive

Theme Verse: "You have captured my heart, my treasure, my bride. You hold it hostage with one glance of your eyes."
— Song of Songs 4:9 (NLT)

A Real Story

I'll be the first to admit, I'm not naturally romantic. I don't remember anniversaries without calendar reminders, I rarely think to buy flowers, and grand gestures don't come naturally to me. For years, I felt guilty about this, thinking I was failing my wife in some fundamental way.

But she surprised me one day when we were talking about what makes her feel loved. "You know what I find romantic?" she said. "When you hold the car door for me. When you bring me coffee without being asked. When you notice I'm tired and suggest I go rest while you handle bedtime."

I was confused. These seemed like basic acts of service, not romance. But as she explained it, romance isn't about the size of the gesture; it's about the intentionality behind it. When I hold her car door, I'm treating her like she's precious to me. When I bring her coffee, I'm thinking about her needs before my own.

To this day, I'm still learning this lesson. Romance for her isn't about expensive dinners or elaborate surprises. It's about the small, consistent ways I show her that she's still the woman who captured my heart, even in the middle of our chaotic, kid-filled life.

The moments when she feels most treasured aren't the planned ones—they're the ordinary Tuesday afternoons when I choose to see her, really see her, and respond to what she needs.

Biblical Reflection

The Song of Songs celebrates romantic love with passionate language, but notice what captures the lover's heart; it's often the small details, the glances, the way she moves through her daily life. Romance isn't just about grand declarations; it's about consistent appreciation.

In the midst of parenting small children, romance can feel like a luxury we can't afford. We're tired, stressed, and focused on survival. But this is precisely when small romantic gestures matter most—they remind both of us that our relationship is more than a parenting partnership.

Romance in this season isn't about recreating your dating days. It's about finding ways to say "you're still beautiful to me" and "I still choose you" in the middle of diaper changes and sleepless nights. It's about protecting the spark that brought you together, even when life feels overwhelming.

When we make these small gestures, we're not just being nice husbands; we're actively nurturing the foundation our entire family is built on.

Family Action Step

This week, identify three small, simple gestures that would make your wife feel seen and appreciated. Ask her directly: "What are some small things I could do that would make you feel loved?" Don't assume you know, let her tell you.

Choose one of these gestures and practice it consistently this week. It might be making her coffee, sending an encouraging text during a hard day, or simply putting your phone away when she's talking to you.

Remember: the goal isn't perfection or constant romance. It's intentionality. Small, consistent gestures often mean more than occasional grand ones.

Reflection Questions

How has your expression of love for your wife changed since becoming a father, and what small adjustments could help her feel more valued in this season?

What does your wife say makes her feel most loved and appreciated, and how can you incorporate more of those gestures into your routine?

Prayer & Blessing

Prayer for This Week

Lord, help me to see my wife through Your eyes, as the treasure You've given me to love and cherish. In the busyness of parenting, don't let me take her for granted or forget to pursue her heart. Show me the small ways I can express my love that will mean the most to her. Give me eyes to notice what she needs and a heart that wants to serve her well. Keep the romance alive in our marriage, not through perfection, but through intentional love. Amen.

Father's Blessing to Speak Over Your Child

Dear child, may you grow up seeing your father cherish and pursue your mother with consistent, thoughtful love. May you learn that real romance isn't found in grand gestures alone, but in the daily choice to treasure someone with your attention and care. And may you understand that a marriage built on small, faithful acts of love creates the secure foundation every family needs. In Jesus' name, amen.

Waiting and Preparing:

For expectant dads still in the waiting phase

WEEK 17

Marveling at the Miracle

"You made all the delicate, inner parts of my body
and knit me together in my mother's womb. Thank you
for making me so wonderfully complex! Your workmanship
is marvelous—how well I know it."
— Psalm 139:13-14 (NLT)

A Real Story

Three of our foster daughters came to us because their mother had Huntington's Disease, a devastating genetic condition that slowly destroys the brain and body. Their mom has since passed away, but the medical reality hung over our family: each girl had a one-in-three chance of carrying the gene. Statistically, one of them should have inherited the disease.

Every morning on my drive to work, I prayed the same prayer: "God, please let all three of them be free from this disease." When each girl turned eighteen and chose to get tested, one by one, the results came back negative. All three girls, against the statistical odds, were completely free from the gene that had taken their mother's life.

Today, I continue to marvel at the miracle of how God not only created them but set them free. Sometimes His greatest miracles are hidden in the very fabric of who our children are, waiting years to be revealed.

Biblical Reflection

David's words in Psalm 139 remind us that God's creative work in our children goes far deeper than what we can observe. As fathers, we often focus on measurable milestones, but God is working miracles we may not discover for years, immune systems that protect them, genetic combinations that make them unique, and neural pathways that will shape their futures.

When we marvel at what God is doing in our children, we develop deeper gratitude and stronger faith. We begin to see them not just as our responsibility to shape, but as God's masterpieces to steward. Even when we can't see the miracles yet, we can trust that God is working in ways that will take our breath away when finally revealed.

Family Action Step

This week, spend time specifically thanking God for the intricate ways He's created each of your children. Look beyond their obvious traits and consider the miraculous complexity of their bodies, minds, and personalities.

Start a prayer journal or mental list of specific things you're asking God to do in your children's lives that you can't yet see—protection from future dangers, preparation for unknown callings, healing from things that haven't even manifested yet.

Take time to simply marvel at your children. Watch them sleep, observe how they think and process the world, and let yourself be amazed by the miracle of their existence.

Reflection Questions

What are you praying for in your children's lives that you can't yet see the results of, and how does trusting God's unseen work change your perspective on their futures?

How might viewing your children as God's intricate masterpieces change the way you parent them day-to-day, especially during challenging moments?

Prayer & Blessing

Prayer for This Week

Father, thank You for the miracle of how You've created my children. Help me to see beyond what I can observe and trust in the marvelous work You're doing in their bodies, minds, and hearts. I pray for protection from dangers I can't even imagine, preparation for purposes I can't yet see, and healing from things that haven't even appeared. Give me faith to believe that You're working miracles in my children that will take my breath away when they're revealed. Help me marvel at Your workmanship in them every day. Amen.

Father's Blessing to Speak Over Your Child

Dear child, you are God's marvelous workmanship, created with intricate care and divine purpose. May you discover throughout your life the miraculous ways God has protected you, prepared you, and set you free from things you never even knew threatened you. May you always marvel at how wonderfully and complex God has made you, and may you trust that He's working miracles in your life that you can't yet see. In Jesus' name, amen.

WEEK 18

Praying Before You Meet

"I knew you before I formed you in your mother's womb. Before you were born I set you apart and appointed you as my prophet to the nations."
— Jeremiah 1:5 (NLT)

A Real Story

It might be too late to start praying for your current child before they were born, but it's never too late to begin praying for the child you have now. And if you're planning for more children, you can start speaking God's promises over them even before conception.

I wish I'd understood this principle earlier in my parenting journey. The power of praying not just for your children, but for people who will be important in their lives long before you meet them. You can start praying for their future spouse before your child can even walk. You can pray for their teachers, their friends, their employers, people who don't even know your child exists yet.

Of our six children, only one is married so far. But I continue to pray for each of their future spouses, even though we've never met five of them. I pray that God is preparing hearts that will love my children well, that He's developing character in young people who will one day become part of our family.

It might sound strange to pray for people you've never met, but God already knows exactly who they are. He's been preparing them just as intentionally as He's been preparing your children. When I pray for my son's future wife, I'm asking God to guard their purity, develop their wisdom, and grow her into a woman of faith. When I pray for my daughters' future husbands, I'm asking God to shape them into men of integrity who will lead with love.

Biblical Reflection

God's words to Jeremiah reveal a profound truth: God knows and plans for our children before they even exist. Their lives aren't accidents or surprises to Him; they're intentional creations with divine purposes. This same principle applies to the people He'll bring into their lives.

When we pray for our children's futures, we're partnering with God's already-existing plans. We're not trying to manipulate outcomes, but aligning our hearts with His purposes for their lives. Our prayers today are investments in relationships and circumstances that won't materialize for years or decades.

This kind of forward-looking prayer develops our faith and changes our perspective on parenting. Instead of just managing today's challenges, we begin to see ourselves as stewards of God's long-term plans for our children's lives.

Family Action Step

This week, begin praying specifically for people who will be important in your children's lives but whom you haven't met yet. Start with their future spouses—pray for their character, their faith, their families, and their marriage preparation.

Expand your prayers to include future teachers, mentors, friends, and employers. Ask God to prepare godly influences and protect your children from harmful relationships.

Write down some of these prayers so you can look back in years to come and see how God answered them. This practice will strengthen both your faith and your children's faith when they see God's faithfulness over time.

Reflection Questions

What would change about your current parenting if you truly believed God has already planned specific people and purposes for your children's futures?

How might praying for your children's future relationships and influences today affect the way you prepare them for those relationships?

Prayer & Blessing

Prayer for This Week

Father, thank You that You knew my children before they were even formed and that You have already planned good purposes for their lives. I pray now for people who will be important in their futures—their future spouses, their mentors, their close friends. Prepare hearts that will love them well and influence them toward You. Guard them from relationships that would harm them and draw them toward people who will encourage their faith. Help me to parent with the long view in mind, knowing that You're preparing them for relationships and purposes I can't yet see. Amen.

Father's Blessing to Speak Over Your Child

Dear child, even before you were born, God had plans for your life and for the people He would bring into it. May you be blessed with friendships that strengthen your faith, mentors who guide you in wisdom, and one day a spouse who loves you as Christ loves the church. May you recognize God's hand in every relationship He brings your way, and may you be a blessing to others just as they are a blessing to you. In Jesus' name, amen.

WEEK 19

Supporting Her Through Everything

"In the same way, you husbands must give honor to your wives. Treat your wife with understanding as you live together. She may be weaker than you are, but she is your equal partner in God's gift of new life. Treat her as you should so your prayers will not be hindered."
— 1 Peter 3:7 (NLT)

A Real Story

It happened during what should have been a routine bedtime. Our toddler was testing every boundary, and my wife had reached her limit after a long day of pregnancy exhaustion. She told him it was time for bed, but he wasn't having it. When she started to raise her voice slightly out of frustration, I saw an opportunity to "help."

"Maybe we should try a different approach," I suggested in front of our son, not thinking about how it sounded. The look on my wife's face told me everything. I had just undermined her authority in front of our child, making her feel unsupported in the exact moment she needed me most.

After we got our son to bed, she quietly but firmly explained what I'd done wrong. "When you disagree with how I'm handling something, we need to discuss it privately later. In front of the kids, I need to know you have my back."

She was absolutely right. Our children need to see us as a united team, especially when one parent is handling discipline or making decisions. If there are disagreements about approach or method, those conversations belong behind closed doors, not in front of impressionable little eyes.

Biblical Reflection

Peter's instruction to treat our wives with understanding goes beyond just being nice to them. The word "understanding" here implies deep knowledge, really knowing what she's dealing with, what she needs, and how our actions affect her.

During pregnancy and early motherhood, our wives are navigating physical exhaustion, hormonal changes, and the overwhelming responsibility of caring for small people. They need to know that we're not just bystanders in parenting, but true partners who will support their decisions publicly and discuss improvements privately.

When we undermine our wives in front of our children, even with good intentions, we damage both our marriage and our family structure. Children need to see their parents as a unified authority, not as competing voices they can play against each other.

Supporting her through everything means being her ally, her advocate, and her backup, especially when she's at her most vulnerable. It means choosing loyalty over being right in the moment.

Family Action Step

This week, commit to the "united front" principle: support your wife's parenting decisions in front of the children, even when you might handle things differently. If you have concerns or suggestions, discuss them privately later.

Practice phrases like "Your mom is right" or "Let's listen to what Mom said" when your wife is handling discipline or instruction. Show your children that you respect her authority and her judgment.

Schedule regular private conversations with your wife about parenting approaches so you can align your strategies without undermining each other in the moment.

Reflection Questions

How do your children currently view your support of their mother's authority, and what adjustments might you need to make to present a more united front?

In what areas of parenting might you and your wife need to have private conversations to better align your approaches and support each other publicly?

Prayer & Blessing

Prayer for This Week

Father, help me to honor my wife by supporting her publicly and discussing our differences privately. Give me wisdom to know when to step in and when to step back, when to lead and when to follow her lead. Make me the kind of husband who strengthens her confidence as a mother rather than undermining it. Help us present a united front to our children while growing together in our parenting approach. Show me how to treat her with the understanding and honor she deserves. Amen.

Father's Blessing to Speak Over Your Child

Dear child, may you grow up seeing your parents support and honor each other, especially in their parenting decisions. May you learn that true love includes loyalty, respect, and unity even when there are disagreements. And may you carry this understanding into your own future relationships, knowing that partnership means being each other's greatest advocates. In Jesus' name, amen.

WEEK 20

Preparing Your Heart

"But Mary kept all these things in her heart and thought about them often."
— Luke 2:19 (NLT)

A Real Story

I was a truck driver with very little children when God began stirring something in my heart about ministry. For months, I felt this growing sense that He was calling me toward something completely different from the life I'd planned. The thought terrified me—how could I provide for my family? What would people think? How could I explain this crazy idea to my wife?

I wrestled with it for months, afraid to even voice what I was feeling. Ministry seemed impossible for someone like me, with my background and our circumstances. But the stirring wouldn't go away. Finally, I worked up the courage to have the conversation I'd been dreading.

"Honey, I think God might be calling me into ministry," I said, bracing myself for confusion, concern, or worse.

Her response stopped me cold: "I know. I've been waiting for you to say it."

She went on to explain that God had been preparing her heart, too, giving her the same sense of calling and purpose. Just like Mary, she had kept these things in her heart and thought about them often, waiting for the right time to see how God would work it all out.

That day I learned that when God prepares our hearts for major life changes, He's often preparing the hearts of those closest to us as well. He doesn't just call individuals—He prepares families for the journey ahead.

Biblical Reflection

Mary's response to the angel's announcement shows us something beautiful about how God prepares hearts for life-changing moments. She didn't just receive the news and move on; she treasured it, pondered it, and let it transform her understanding of what God was doing.

As fathers preparing for new children or major life transitions, we need this same heart posture. God often begins preparing us months or even years before the significant moments arrive. The stirrings we feel, the dreams that won't go away, the growing sense of responsibility or calling—these are often God's way of getting our hearts ready for what's coming.

Sometimes this preparation feels overwhelming or scary. We wonder if we're hearing God correctly or if we're capable of what He's asking. But Mary's example reminds us that God's preparations are thorough. He's not just working on our hearts—He's orchestrating circumstances and preparing others who will walk alongside us.

The key is learning to treasure and ponder what God is doing rather than rushing ahead or shrinking back in fear.

Family Action Step

This week, take time to honestly assess what God might be stirring in your heart about your family's future. Are there dreams, concerns, or callings that keep coming up that you haven't yet discussed with your wife?

Create space for unhurried conversation with your spouse about what God might be preparing both of you for. Listen for how He might already be working in her heart about the same things.

Start keeping a simple journal of the things God is stirring in your heart so you can look back and see how He was preparing you for changes or challenges that hadn't yet materialized.

Reflection Questions

What has God been stirring in your heart about your role as a father or your family's future that you haven't yet fully embraced or discussed?

How might God be using this season of your life to prepare you for responsibilities, opportunities, or challenges you can't yet see clearly?

Prayer & Blessing

Prayer for This Week

Father, thank You for how gently and thoroughly You prepare our hearts for the changes and challenges ahead. Help me to treasure and ponder the things You're stirring in my spirit rather than rushing ahead in fear or shrinking back in doubt. Give me wisdom to recognize Your voice and courage to follow where You're leading. Prepare not just my heart, but my family's hearts for whatever You have planned for us. Make me sensitive to what You're already doing in my wife's heart and in our circumstances. Amen.

Father's Blessing to Speak Over Your Child

Dear child, may your heart always be sensitive to God's stirring and preparation in your life. May you learn to treasure and ponder the things God shows you, trusting that He is always preparing you for the good plans He has for your future. And may you have the faith to follow where He leads, knowing that His preparations are always perfect and His timing is always right. In Jesus' name, amen.

Those First Days:

Surviving and thriving with a newborn

WEEK 21

Hello, Little One

"And you will recognize him by this sign: You will find a baby wrapped snugly in strips of cloth, lying in a manger."
— Luke 2:12 (NLT)

A Real Story

When my son was born, I was completely unaware of how serious everything had become. My wife was in tremendous pain, and looking back, I realize she almost died during that delivery. But the medical team never fully communicated the gravity of the situation to me in the moment. I was focused entirely on what I could see—the miracle unfolding before my eyes.

Then I heard his first cry, and everything else faded into the background. The nurses placed this tiny, perfect person in my arms, and I was completely overwhelmed. His fingers were so small they could barely wrap around one of mine. His eyes blinked open, trying to focus on this bright new world he'd just entered.

Getting to hold him for the first time was the most precious moment I have ever experienced. Nothing had prepared me for the rush of love, protectiveness, and wonder that flooded my heart as I looked down at this little person who was now my son. In that instant, everything changed. I wasn't just a husband anymore—I was somebody's father.

I whispered, "Hello, little one," and felt the full weight of what God had just entrusted to me. This tiny life, completely dependent and perfectly formed, was now my responsibility to love, protect, and guide. It was terrifying and beautiful all at once.

Biblical Reflection

The angel's announcement to the shepherds gives us a beautiful picture of how God reveals Himself through the vulnerability of a newborn. The sign wasn't a mighty display of power, but a baby "wrapped snugly" and lying in humble circumstances. There's something profoundly sacred about those first moments of meeting your child.

When we hold our newborns for the first time, we're experiencing an echo of how God sees us, with overwhelming love, fierce protectiveness, and unlimited hope for the future. The helplessness that initially overwhelms us as new fathers is actually a gift; it reminds us of our complete dependence on God for wisdom, strength, and guidance in this new role.

Those first moments of meeting your child are holy ground. All the preparation, all the worry, all the anticipation culminate in this sacred introduction. Like the shepherds who found exactly what the angel had promised, we find in our children a miracle that changes everything about how we see ourselves and our purpose.

Family Action Step

If you're still waiting for your child's arrival, take time this week to prepare your heart for that first meeting. Consider what you want to say to them, how you want to pray over them, and what promises you want to make to God about how you'll steward this precious life.

If your child is already here, revisit those first moments in your mind. Write down what you remember about holding them for the first time, what you felt, and what you promised them. Keep this record to share with them someday.

Take time to hold your child, even if they're not a newborn anymore, and remember the sacredness of what God has given you.

Reflection Questions

What do you hope to feel and experience in those first moments of meeting your child, and how do you want to prepare your heart for that encounter?

How might viewing your child's birth as a sacred moment, like the shepherds finding the Christ child, change your perspective on the responsibility you're receiving?

Prayer & Blessing

Prayer for This Week

Father, thank You for the incredible gift of new life and for the sacred privilege of being entrusted with one of Your children. Prepare my heart for those first precious moments of meeting my son or daughter. Help me to see them through Your eyes—with overwhelming love and unlimited hope for their future. Give me wisdom to steward this sacred responsibility well and strength to protect and guide them throughout their life. May I never lose the wonder of those first moments when everything changed. Amen.

Father's Blessing to Speak Over Your Child

Dear little one, you are fearfully and wonderfully made, a precious gift from God placed into our family's care. From the moment we first held you, our hearts were forever changed. May you always know how wanted you are, how loved you are, and how great God's plans are for your life. May you grow in wisdom and stature and in favor with God and others. Welcome to the world, precious child. In Jesus' name, amen.

WEEK 22

Grace at 3 AM

"The faithful love of the Lord never ends!
His mercies begin afresh each morning. Great is
his faithfulness; his mercies begin afresh each day."
— Lamentations 3:22-23 (NLT)

A Real Story

I got used to the middle-of-the-night wake-ups with our son, who wasn't the healthiest baby. Ear infections, breathing issues, and feeding problems. It seemed like something was always disrupting his sleep, which meant it was always disrupting ours. After months of this routine, I'd developed an almost automatic response to his cries.

One particular night, I woke up in the rocking chair with my son peacefully in my arms. I had absolutely no memory of getting up, walking to his room, picking him up, or settling into the chair. One moment, I was asleep in my bed, the next I was holding my quiet, content baby in the darkened nursery.

I sat there for a moment, completely bewildered. How did I get here? How long had we been sitting like this? My son was sleeping soundly, his breathing steady and peaceful. Whatever had woken him up had been resolved without my even being consciously aware of it.

That was definitely grace at 3 AM. God had somehow carried me through the motions of comforting my child while I was essentially sleepwalking. In my exhaustion, when I had nothing left to give, He provided what was needed, for both my son and for me.

It was a tangible reminder that even when we're running on empty, God's mercies are new every morning, and sometimes they show up in the middle of the night, too.

Biblical Reflection

Jeremiah wrote about God's new mercies during one of the darkest periods of his life, and his words take on special meaning during those exhausting early months of fatherhood. When we're surviving on broken sleep and running on fumes, we need fresh mercy not just each morning, but sometimes each hour.

Those 3 AM moments with our children aren't just interruptions to our rest—they're opportunities to experience God's faithful love in the most depleted moments of our lives. When we have nothing left to give, He provides the strength to get up one more time, the patience to comfort one more cry, the love to keep serving when we're completely spent.

The beauty of God's grace is that it doesn't depend on our energy levels or our emotional state. His mercies are new even at 3 AM, even when we're barely conscious, even when we're not sure how we're functioning. He meets us in our weakness and provides exactly what we need.

These midnight moments of grace become precious memories—evidence of God's faithfulness during a season that tests us physically, emotionally, and spiritually.

Family Action Step

This week, when you're woken up in the middle of the night (and you probably will be), try to see it as an opportunity to experience God's fresh mercy rather than just an interruption to your sleep.

In those quiet moments with your child, take a moment to thank God for His faithfulness and ask Him to give you whatever you need—patience, energy, peace, or just the ability to function. Look for small evidence of His grace during the exhausting times.

Keep a mental note of moments when God provides strength you didn't think you had or peace in the midst of chaos. These become testimonies of His faithfulness that you'll treasure later.

Reflection Questions

How have you experienced God's grace during the most exhausting moments of fatherhood, and what has that taught you about His faithfulness?

What would change about those middle-of-the-night moments if you viewed them as opportunities to experience God's mercy rather than just disruptions to your rest?

Prayer & Blessing

Prayer for This Week

Father, thank You that Your mercies are new, not just each morning, but throughout the night when I need them most. When I'm exhausted and running on empty, provide the grace I need to love and serve my family well. Help me to see those 3 AM moments not as burdens, but as opportunities to experience Your faithful love in my weakness. Give me strength when I have none, patience when I'm depleted, and peace when everything feels overwhelming. Show me Your presence in the quiet, difficult hours. Amen.

Father's Blessing to Speak Over Your Child

Dear child, may you always know that you are worth every sacrifice, every sleepless night, and every moment of exhaustion. May you see in your father's willingness to care for you at all hours a picture of how your Heavenly Father never sleeps and is always ready to meet your needs. And may you grow up understanding that God's love and mercy are available to you every moment of every day and night. In Jesus' name, amen.

WEEK 23

The Power of Your Touch

"Then he took the children in his arms and placed his hands on their heads and blessed them."
— Mark 10:16 (NLT)

A Real Story

I developed a habit early on of taking each of our babies and holding them against my chest, skin-to-skin when possible, or simply carrying them around the house while carefully supporting their neck. There was something profound about those moments—feeling their tiny heartbeat against mine, their small body trusting completely in my strength to keep them safe.

At first, I worried I wasn't doing it right. My hands felt so large compared to their delicate frames. What if I held them too tight? What if I didn't support them properly? But I soon discovered that my gentle touch was creating something beautiful—a bonding experience that established an early emotional connection between us.

Those quiet moments of holding them close became sacred time. Sometimes they would fall asleep to the rhythm of my breathing. Other times, they would just look up at me with those wide, curious eyes, taking in this big person who was learning to be their dad. I could feel trust building between us with every careful touch.

I learned that my hands—these same hands that worked hard jobs and handled tough tasks—could also communicate tenderness, safety, and love. The way I held them was their first experience of what it meant to be cherished and protected by their father.

Years later, some of my most treasured memories are of those simple moments when my touch was all they needed to feel secure in an overwhelming world.

Biblical Reflection

When Jesus blessed the children, He didn't just speak words over them—He took them in His arms and placed His hands on them. There's something powerful about physical touch that communicates love, blessing, and acceptance in ways words alone cannot.

As fathers, our touch carries tremendous power. For our children, especially in those early months, our gentle hands represent safety, comfort, and unconditional love. The way we hold them, support them, and care for them through touch becomes their first experience of being valued and cherished.

Your touch as a father has the potential to communicate God's love in tangible ways. When you carefully support your baby's head, gently stroke their back, or simply hold them close, you're giving them a physical representation of how their Heavenly Father holds them with perfect love and protection.

This kind of gentle, nurturing touch from fathers helps establish emotional security and trust that will influence how our children relate to others throughout their lives. It's a powerful responsibility and a beautiful privilege.

Family Action Step

This week, be intentional about gentle, nurturing touch with your child. If you have a newborn, spend time holding them skin-to-skin or simply carrying them around while supporting their head and neck. Notice how they respond to your careful touch.

If your children are older, look for appropriate ways to show affection through touch, a hand on their shoulder, a gentle hug, or ruffling their hair. Pay attention to how your touch can communicate love and security.

Take time during these moments of physical closeness to pray silently over your child, asking God to bless them and to use your touch to communicate His love to their heart.

Reflection Questions

How does your gentle touch with your children reflect the way God holds and cares for you, and what does this teach you about fatherhood?

What memories do you want your children to have of how their father's hands treated them, and how can you be intentional about creating those memories?

Prayer & Blessing

Prayer for This Week

Father, thank You for the privilege of communicating Your love through my touch. Help my hands to be gentle, careful, and nurturing with my children. Show me how to use appropriate physical affection to build security and trust. May my touch always communicate safety, love, and blessing. Give me wisdom to know how to hold them, comfort them, and show them through my careful care what it means to be cherished. Make my touch a reflection of how You hold each of us with perfect love. Amen.

Father's Blessing to Speak Over Your Child

Dear child, may you always remember the safety and love you felt in your father's arms. May the gentle way he holds and cares for you give you a picture of how your Heavenly Father holds you with perfect love and protection. And may you carry that sense of being cherished and valued with you throughout your life, knowing that you are precious and loved beyond measure. In Jesus' name, amen.

WEEK 24

Speaking Life Over Your Baby

"The tongue can bring death or life; those who love to talk will reap the consequences."
— Proverbs 18:21 (NLT)

A Real Story

I grew up in a home where words weren't always kind. With parents who struggled with alcohol, much of what I heard growing up wasn't encouraging or life-giving. Instead of words that built me up, I often heard words that tore me down. And for a long time, I believed them.

When I became a father, I made a decision: things would be different for my children. Whether they were foster kids coming into my home for a season or my own biological kids, I wanted them to hear something different when they listened to their dad. I wanted my words to give them life.

So I started speaking encouragement, sometimes small things, like telling them I was proud of how they tried, or reminding them that they were loved no matter what. Other times it was bigger—calling out their strengths, noticing their kindness, or telling them that God had a purpose for their lives.

Over the years, I've watched those words take root. Each of my children, whether here for a time or forever, has grown into someone I'm proud of. I believe that part of that is because they had a father who chose to use his words to build, not break.

It doesn't mean I've been perfect, but it does mean I've been intentional. And when I look at them now, I see what the Bible promised: words really can shape a future.

Biblical Reflection

Scripture reminds us that our words carry tremendous power, power to bring death or life. As fathers, the way we speak to our children can leave lasting marks on their hearts. Words can either wound and create insecurity, or they can encourage and build a foundation of confidence and love.

When Jesus spoke, His words brought healing, peace, and hope. He told people who felt forgotten that they were seen. He told sinners they were forgiven. He spoke blessings, truth, and life into everyone He encountered.

In the same way, our children need to hear words from us that affirm who they are and who God made them to be. Every "I love you," every "I'm proud of you," every "You can do this" is like planting seeds of life that will grow for years to come.

Your words can become the soundtrack your children replay in their minds when life gets tough. If those words are full of encouragement, faith, and love, they'll carry your children forward with strength and security.

Family Action Step

This week, be intentional with the words you speak to your children. If your baby is still little, speak blessings over them as you hold them. Tell them they are loved, cherished, and chosen by God, even if they can't understand your words yet; they can still feel the tone of your voice.

If your children are older, go out of your way to encourage them. Notice something they're doing well and say it out loud. Tell them you're proud of them. Remind them that God has a plan for their lives.

And as you speak these words, remember that you are giving them a gift that lasts far beyond the moment, it's a gift they can carry with them for a lifetime.

Reflection Questions

What kinds of words did you grow up hearing, and how have they shaped you?

What kind of "word legacy" do you want to leave for your children, and how can you start speaking that into them today?

Prayer & Blessing

Prayer for This Week

Father, thank You for giving me the power to speak life through my words. Forgive me for the times I've used words carelessly. Help me to be intentional in speaking encouragement, truth, and love to my children. May my words reflect Your heart and plant seeds of hope, faith, and joy in their lives. Teach me to use my voice to bless and not to curse, to build up and not to tear down. Amen.

Father's Blessing to Speak Over Your Child

Dear child, may you always hear words of life spoken over you. May your heart be filled with confidence because you know you are deeply loved and wonderfully made. May my words remind you of your value and point you toward the incredible purpose God has for your life. And may you never doubt that you are cherished, capable, and precious in God's sight. In Jesus' name, amen.

Building Connection:

Creating lasting bonds with your child

WEEK 25

The Gift of Being Present

"Then he said, 'I tell you the truth, unless you turn
from your sins and become like little children,
you will never get into the Kingdom of Heaven.'"
— Matthew 18:3 (NLT)

A Real Story

I'll never forget the moment our son took his first steps, mainly because his first steps weren't really steps at all. They were in the form of running.

Because of sickness and hospital stays, we hadn't seen him roll over, crawl, or cruise along the furniture like most babies do. He was always just content to sit and watch the world go by. The doctors never seemed overly concerned, so we tried to trust their reassurance. Still, I often wondered if he would ever find his stride.

Then one day, at a family reunion, everything changed. Surrounded by cousins and other kids his age, something clicked inside him. He saw them running around and decided he wanted to join in. And just like that, without warning or practice, he was up on his feet, running. No slow steps, no wobbly crawl-to-walk transition, just pure movement.

We stood there in awe, watching this little boy who had faced so many challenges suddenly break into his own kind of freedom. It was such an amazing gift to witness it in person. That moment reminded me how precious it is to simply be present, to be there when the unexpected, extraordinary things happen.

Biblical Reflection

Jesus often pointed to children as examples of how we're called to live, with openness, simplicity, and wonder. Babies and young children don't worry much about yesterday or tomorrow. They live fully in the present, finding joy in what's right in front of them.

As fathers, it's easy to let our minds be consumed by work, stress, or distractions. But our children need us to be fully present, with our eyes, our ears, and our hearts. Moments like a first laugh, a first word, or even a first step can't be recaptured. They're gifts from God, reminders of His goodness, and glimpses of His Kingdom breaking into our everyday lives.

Being present doesn't mean you have to create big, dramatic moments. It simply means showing up—putting down your phone, slowing down your pace, and noticing the little things your child is discovering. Sometimes the greatest gift you can give your child is not your advice or your resources, but your undivided attention.

Family Action Step

This week, be intentional about being fully present with your child. If your baby is small, spend time watching their expressions, listening to their sounds, and responding with joy. If your child is older, join them in their world, play with them, listen to their stories, or go on a simple walk together without distractions.

Don't underestimate how much your presence communicates love and security. Your child will remember the times you were with them more than the things you bought or planned for them.

Reflection Questions

What distractions most often keep you from being fully present with your children?

How can you create more intentional moments of connection this week where your child has your full attention?

Prayer & Blessing

Prayer for This Week

Father, thank You for the precious gift of my child and the moments You give us together. Help me not to take those moments for granted. Teach me to slow down, set aside distractions, and truly be present. May my child feel my love through my attention and presence, and may these moments reflect the way You are always present with us. Amen.

Father's Blessing to Speak Over Your Child

Dear child, may you always know that your father delights in being with you. May my presence remind you that you are valuable, seen, and worth every moment of my time. And may you carry the assurance throughout your life that just as your earthly father has been with you, your Heavenly Father is always near—faithful, attentive, and full of love. In Jesus' name, amen.

WEEK 26

Play as Worship

"A time to cry and a time to laugh.
A time to grieve and a time to dance."
— Ecclesiastes 3:4 (NLT)

A Real Story

Board games have always been a big part of our family life. Even now, our favorite go-to game is Scotland Yard, where the challenge is to track down the elusive Mister X. Every child wanted their chance to be Mister X, sneaking around the board, laughing as the rest of us scrambled to figure out where they were hiding.

It wasn't just Scotland Yard. Over the years, there was always room for fun in our family. From "pin the tail on the donkey" at birthday parties to our very own creative Easter egg hunts, laughter filled the air. We even made up our own version of soccer where the whistle didn't always blow when someone used their hands, the rules were bent a little, but the joy never stopped.

Those playful times became part of our family culture—moments when joy brought us closer together and gave us memories we still talk about today. What I've realized is that those silly games and times of fun weren't just entertainment. They were reminders of God's goodness. They created spaces for joy, laughter, and connection that reflected something deeply spiritual.

Biblical Reflection

The writer of Ecclesiastes reminds us that life is full of different seasons and rhythms. There's a time to cry and a time to laugh. A time to grieve and a time to dance. Our God is not a God of only seriousness and solemnity—He also delights in joy, play, and laughter.

As fathers, one of the ways we reflect God's heart to our children is by entering into their joy. When we take time to play, laugh, and be silly, we're not just passing time; we're showing our kids that life with God is full, rich, and overflowing with joy.

Jesus Himself welcomed children and delighted in their presence. Children naturally play, imagine, and laugh, and when we join them in those moments, we step into something that honors God. Play becomes a kind of worship, a way of celebrating the gift of life He's given us.

Family Action Step

This week, set aside intentional time for play. If your child is little, get on the floor with them, play peek-a-boo, or make silly faces that make them giggle. If your children are older, pull out a favorite board game, organize a family game night, or do something active and fun together.

Don't worry about winning or losing, the goal isn't the game itself, but the joy you share. Use these moments to remind your children that laughter and fun are gifts from God, and that He delights in seeing His children filled with joy.

Reflection Questions

How can you invite more joy and laughter into your home this week?

In what ways does your willingness to play with your children reflect God's delight in you?

Prayer & Blessing

Prayer for This Week

Father, thank You for the gift of joy and laughter. Teach me to embrace play as part of my worship to You. Help me to set aside distractions and take time to laugh and enjoy life with my children. May our home be filled with moments of fun that remind us of Your goodness and draw us closer together. Amen.

Father's Blessing to Speak Over Your Child

Dear child, may your life always be filled with joy and laughter. May our times of play remind you that God delights in your happiness. And may you grow up knowing that life with your Heavenly Father is not only full of purpose, but also full of joy, wonder, and delight. In Jesus' name, amen.

WEEK 27

Bedtime Stories and Bible Truth

"We will not hide these truths from our children;
we will tell the next generation about the glorious deeds
of the Lord, about his power and his mighty wonders."
— Psalm 78:4 (NLT)

A Real Story

I've already shared how my kids still remember those Chronicles of Narnia bedtime stories, the different voices I used for each character, the way I tried to make the adventures come alive in our darkened bedroom. Years later, they don't remember most of my parenting lectures, but they can still quote entire passages from those books because of how we experienced them together.

I would do the same with Bible stories. David fighting Goliath got the full treatment. A young, determined voice for David, a booming, threatening voice for the giant. Daniel in the lion's den became an adventure story with suspense and drama. The disciples on the stormy sea got voices filled with panic until Jesus spoke peace over the waves.

Suddenly, Bible time wasn't something to endure; it was something to anticipate. My kids started asking for specific stories: "Dad, tell us the one about Moses and the burning bush again, but do the voice!" They weren't just hearing Bible facts; they were experiencing Bible truth in ways that stuck in their hearts and minds.

Now that they're grown, guess what they remember most vividly from their childhood faith formation? Not the formal devotions or the theological explanations. It's the way their dad made God's word come alive through story and voice and shared excitement.

Biblical Reflection

The psalmist understood that faith gets passed down through storytelling, not just instruction. When we tell our children about God's mighty deeds, we're not just teaching facts; we're inviting them into a grand narrative that they're part of.

Making Bible stories engaging and memorable isn't about entertainment for entertainment's sake. It's about helping our children see that God's word is alive, powerful, and relevant to their lives. When we bring creativity and enthusiasm to Bible time, we communicate that these stories matter deeply to us.

Children remember what captures their imagination. If we present Bible truth as boring or burdensome, that's how they'll view God's word. But if we make it come alive through voices, drama, and genuine excitement, we help them fall in love with the stories that will shape their faith for life.

Our enthusiasm for God's word becomes contagious, creating positive associations with Scripture that will serve them well when they're old enough to read and study it on their own.

Family Action Step

This week, choose one Bible story to tell your child (or children) using voices, drama, and creative storytelling. Even if your child is still a baby, practice reading Bible stories aloud with expression and enthusiasm.

Don't worry about being perfect or professional—focus on making the story engaging and memorable. Let your excitement about God's word show through your voice and energy.

Consider starting a rotation of favorite Bible stories that you tell regularly, developing character voices and dramatic elements that will make them stick in your children's minds and hearts.

Reflection Questions

How do you currently share Bible stories with your children, and what could you do to make God's word more engaging and memorable for them?

What Bible stories from your own childhood do you remember most vividly, and what made them stick in your memory?

Prayer & Blessing

Prayer for This Week

Father, give me creativity and enthusiasm as I share Your word with my children. Help me to make Bible stories come alive in ways that capture their imagination and plant seeds of faith deep in their hearts. Show me how to be a storyteller who helps my children fall in love with Your truth. May my excitement about Your word become contagious, creating positive associations with Scripture that will last their entire lives. Use these simple moments of storytelling to build a foundation of faith that nothing can shake. Amen.

Father's Blessing to Speak Over Your Child

Dear child, may God's word come alive in your heart through the stories your father tells you. May you grow up loving the Bible not as a burden to carry, but as an adventure to live. And may these early experiences with God's truth create a hunger in you to know Him more deeply throughout your entire life. In Jesus' name, amen.

WEEK 28

Celebrating Every Small Victory

"Always be joyful. Never stop praying.
Be thankful in all circumstances, for this is God's
will for you who belong to Christ Jesus."
— 1 Thessalonians 5:16-18 (NLT)

A Real Story

I made a decision early in my parenting that I would focus more on celebrating what my children did right than punishing what they did wrong. It wasn't always easy; sometimes, bad behavior demands immediate attention, but I was determined to make sure they knew when they pleased me.

Good marks on school reports earned little prizes, nothing expensive, just something to mark the achievement. When they helped around the house without being asked, I made sure they knew I noticed. When they showed kindness to their siblings, I celebrated it as if they'd just won a championship.

The decision came from my own childhood. I never heard the words "I'm proud of you" growing up, and I knew how much that absence had affected me. I was determined that my children would never wonder whether their father was proud of them or pleased with who they were becoming.

Now that they're grown, they tell me those celebrations and affirmations shaped how they see themselves. They learned that their father was watching for their successes, not just their failures, and that made them want to give him more reasons to be proud.

Biblical Reflection

Paul's instruction to "always be joyful" and "be thankful in all circumstances" seems impossible until we realize it's about choosing to focus on what God is doing rather than what's going wrong. As fathers, this perspective transforms how we see our children's growth and development.

Every small milestone, first smiles, attempts to roll over, baby's first words, represents God's intricate plan unfolding in our children's lives. When we celebrate these moments with genuine joy and gratitude, we're acknowledging God's faithful work and teaching our children that growth and effort are worth celebrating.

Children thrive when they know their fathers are watching for their successes, not just their mistakes. Our celebration of their small victories builds their confidence, shapes their identity, and creates an atmosphere of encouragement that helps them take healthy risks and keep trying when things are difficult.

When we make a bigger deal about what they do right than what they do wrong, we're reflecting God's heart toward us—a Father who celebrates our growth and delights in our progress.

Family Action Step

This week, commit to celebrating at least one small victory or positive behavior in your child each day. If your child is a newborn, celebrate developmental milestones like longer periods of alertness, better sleep patterns, or successful feeding sessions.

For older children, look for character qualities, kind actions, or effort rather than just achievements. Make your celebrations specific: "I noticed how patient you were with your little brother today" rather than just "good job."

Tell your child regularly that you're proud of them, especially if these weren't words you heard growing up. Break the cycle and make sure your children never wonder whether their father delights in them.

Reflection Questions

What small victories and positive behaviors in your children might you be overlooking because you're focused on correction and discipline?

How might your regular celebration of your children's growth and character affect their willingness to try new things and persevere through challenges?

Prayer & Blessing

Prayer for This Week

Father, help me to see my children through Your eyes—focusing on their growth, their effort, and their developing character rather than just their mistakes. Give me a heart that celebrates small victories and finds joy in everyday moments of progress. Show me how to encourage them with words and celebrations that build their confidence and identity. May my delight in them reflect Your delight in us as Your children. Help me to be quick to affirm and slow to criticize. Amen.

Father's Blessing to Speak Over Your Child

Dear child, may you always know how proud your father is of you—not just for your achievements, but for your heart, your effort, and the unique way God has made you. May you grow up confident in your father's love and approval, knowing that you bring him joy simply by being who you are. And may this foundation of celebration and affirmation give you courage to become everything God has created you to be. In Jesus' name, amen.

Practical Parenting:

Day-to-day wisdom for raising kids

WEEK 29

Discipline That Builds Up

"Start children off on the way they should go,
and even when they are old they will not turn from it."
— Proverbs 22:6 (NLT)

A Real Story

There was a season when our daughter had walked away from everything we'd taught her about faith. She'd gotten involved with drugs and a destructive relationship, and seemed determined to reject every value we'd tried to instill. She was old enough that she no longer wanted to listen to our advice or guidance.

Her mother and I could only pray for her every day, trusting that the foundation we'd built during her childhood would somehow hold, even when we couldn't see any evidence of it. We watched from a distance as she made choices that broke our hearts, feeling helpless to protect her from consequences we could see coming.

But God was working even when we couldn't see it. Today, she's in Bible college, married to a wonderful African man, and hoping to one day serve as a pastor and missionary. When she tells her testimony of what drew her back to the Lord, she always mentions the same thing: growing up in a loving home with believing parents and wanting to find that same peace she remembered from childhood.

The discipline and boundaries we'd established weren't just rules to follow—they had created an atmosphere of safety and love that she missed when she was living in chaos. The foundation we'd built through years of loving correction had given her something to return to when the world proved unreliable.

She didn't come back because we were perfect parents, but because we'd created a home where grace was larger than mistakes and love was stronger than rebellion.

Biblical Reflection

Solomon's promise about training children carries both hope and patience. The "way they should go" isn't just about behavior modification; it's about building character and creating an internal compass that will guide them when external authority is no longer present.

Effective discipline builds rather than tears down. It creates security rather than fear, understanding rather than compliance. When our correction comes from love rather than anger, it establishes a foundation of trust that can withstand even seasons of rebellion.

The goal of discipline isn't just immediate obedience, but long-term character formation. We're not just managing behavior; we're shaping hearts and minds that will one day make independent choices about faith, relationships, and values.

Sometimes the fruit of our discipline doesn't appear for years. Children who seem to reject everything we've taught may eventually return to the foundation we built, recognizing it as a source of peace and stability they can't find anywhere else.

Family Action Step

This week, evaluate your approach to discipline with your current children. Ask yourself whether your correction builds up their character or just manages their behavior. Focus on discipline that teaches rather than just punishes.

When you need to correct your child, explain not just what they did wrong, but why the right choice matters for their character and their relationships. Help them understand that boundaries exist because they're loved, not because they're bad.

Pray specifically for the long-term impact of your discipline, trusting that you're building something that will serve them well even when you're not around to guide them.

Reflection Questions

How do you want your children to remember the discipline and correction they received in your home, and what adjustments might you need to make to create those memories?

What "way" are you training your children to go that you hope they'll carry with them even when they're making independent choices as adults?

Prayer & Blessing

Prayer for This Week

Father, give me wisdom to discipline my children in ways that build their character rather than just control their behavior. Help me to correct them from love, not anger, and to create boundaries that communicate safety rather than restriction. When they struggle or rebel, remind me that I'm building a foundation they can return to, not just managing today's problems. Give me the patience to trust that the training I'm providing now will serve them well when they're old enough to choose their own path. Amen.

Father's Blessing to Speak Over Your Child

Dear child, may the discipline and boundaries in our home always communicate how much you are loved and valued. May the foundation we're building together give you security, confidence, and wisdom that will guide you throughout your life. And even if you ever walk away from what we've taught you, may you always know there's a home of grace and love waiting for your return. In Jesus' name, amen.

WEEK 30

Consistency When You're Tired

"So, my dear brothers and sisters, be strong and immovable. Always work enthusiastically for the Lord, for you know that nothing you do for the Lord is ever useless."
— 1 Corinthians 15:58 (NLT)

A Real Story

I remember another man from our church approaching me one Sunday with a look of genuine amazement. "I saw your wife at the grocery store with all your children," he said, "and they were walking in a perfect row behind her. How is that even possible?"

I could tell you exactly how it was possible: consistent parenting. Together as a couple, my wife and I had established routines and boundaries that mattered to us, and we stuck to them even when it was hard, even when we were tired, even when it would have been easier to let things slide.

Those grocery store trips didn't happen by accident. They were the result of countless practice sessions at home, clear expectations about public behavior, and follow-through on consequences when boundaries were crossed. It meant sometimes leaving a cart full of groceries to take a child outside for correction. It meant maintaining standards even when we were exhausted.

The beautiful thing was that once our children knew the boundaries were real and consistent, they actually felt more secure within them. They didn't have to guess what was expected or test limits constantly because they knew we meant what we said.

Biblical Reflection

Paul's call to be "strong and immovable" takes on special meaning in parenting. When we're exhausted and overwhelmed, the temptation is to let standards slip, to ignore small infractions, or to take the path of least resistance. But consistent boundaries are actually gifts we give our children.

Children thrive with predictable routines and reliable expectations. When they know what's expected and can trust that boundaries will be maintained, they feel secure enough to explore, grow, and develop within those safe parameters.

Consistency in parenting isn't about perfection or rigidity; it's about being dependable. Our children need to know that their father's word means something, that love and discipline go together, and that family rules exist to create safety, not restriction.

The beautiful truth is that nothing we do for the Lord—including the daily grind of consistent parenting—is ever useless. Every time we follow through when we're tired, every boundary we maintain when it's inconvenient, we're building something that will serve our children for life.

Family Action Step

This week, identify one area where you've been inconsistent with boundaries or routines because it's been easier to let things slide. Choose to re-establish that expectation and commit to following through, even when you're tired.

Work with your wife to ensure you're both consistent with the same rules and routines. Children feel most secure when both parents maintain the same expectations.

Remember that consistency doesn't mean perfection. When you slip up or make mistakes, acknowledge them and get back on track. Your children need to see that consistency is about commitment, not flawlessness.

Reflection Questions

Where have you been inconsistent with boundaries or routines because it felt easier in the moment, and how has that affected your children's behavior and security?

What would your children say about whether they can depend on your word and your follow-through, and what adjustments might you need to make?

Prayer & Blessing

Prayer for This Week

Father, give me the strength to be consistent in my parenting even when I'm tired, and it would be easier to let things slide. Help me to see that the boundaries and routines I maintain are gifts that create security for my children. Give my wife and me unity in our expectations and follow-through. When I'm tempted to take shortcuts or ignore small infractions, remind me that consistency builds trust and safety. Help me to be dependable in both my love and my discipline. Amen.

Father's Blessing to Speak Over Your Child

Dear child, may you always feel the security that comes from knowing what is expected and that your parents' word can be trusted. May the consistent love and boundaries in our home give you confidence to grow and explore within safe parameters. And may you learn that true freedom comes not from the absence of boundaries, but from the security of knowing you are loved unconditionally within them. In Jesus' name, amen.

WEEK 31

Being the Example

"Don't let anyone think less of you because you are y oung. Be an example to all believers in what you say, in the way you live, in your love, your faith, and your purity."
— 1 Timothy 4:12 (NLT)

A Real Story

I quickly realized when my son was a toddler that he would impersonate everything I did. He wanted to hold tools when I was working on projects. He'd pretend to shave in the bathroom mirror while I was getting ready for work. He copied my mannerisms, my expressions, even the way I walked across the room.

That's when it hit me how important it was to be the example, not just give instructions. My father's favorite phrase had been "Do as I say, not as I do," and while it worked to some degree, I had to learn many life lessons the hard way because of the inconsistency between his words and his actions.

I decided I didn't want my children to have to figure out which version of their father to follow, the one who gave good advice or the one whose behavior told a different story. If I were going to teach them about integrity, I needed to demonstrate it. If I wanted them to respect others, they needed to see me treating people with respect, especially their mother.

The weight of being constantly watched and imitated was initially overwhelming. Every word, every reaction, every choice was being absorbed by these little sponges who would eventually reproduce what they observed more than what they heard.

But it also became a gift. Knowing my children were watching made me more intentional about the man I wanted to be, not just the father I wanted to appear to be.

Biblical Reflection

Paul's instruction to Timothy about being an example applies powerfully to fatherhood. Our children don't just need our teaching—they need our modelling. They're learning how to be human by watching how we handle frustration, treat others, respond to stress, and live out our faith.

The phrase "in what you say, in the way you live, in your love, your faith, and your purity" covers every aspect of character our children are observing. They're learning what men look like when they're angry, how husbands treat wives, how believers respond to disappointment, and how fathers handle responsibility.

Children are natural imitators. They will reproduce our patterns, our reactions, and our character long before they understand our explanations. This means our daily choices—how we speak to our wives, how we handle setbacks, how we treat service workers—are actually parenting decisions.

The goal isn't perfection, but authenticity. When we make mistakes, our children need to see how we handle confession, forgiveness, and growth. Even our failures can become teaching moments when we model humility and repentance.

Family Action Step

This week, pay attention to what your child is observing and potentially imitating from your behavior. Watch how they play or interact with others—you might be surprised to see yourself reflected in their actions.

Choose one area where you want to be a better example for your children. It might be how you speak to your wife, how you handle frustration, or how you prioritize your relationship with God. Focus on modelling the behavior you want to see from them.

Remember that your children are learning more from your consistency than from your perfection. Be the same person in public and private, in easy moments and stressful ones.

Reflection Questions

What behaviors or attitudes are your children likely learning from watching you, and which of these make you proud versus concerned?

If your children grow up to parent exactly like you parent, treat their spouses exactly like you treat yours, and handle stress exactly like you do, how would that make you feel?

Prayer & Blessing

Prayer for This Week

Father, help me to understand the weight and privilege of being an example to my children. Make me the same man in private that I am in public, the same father in easy moments that I am in difficult ones. Show me where my actions don't match my words, and give me the integrity to change. Help me to model the character, faith, and love that I want to see reproduced in my children. When I fail, teach me to handle it with humility and grace. Amen.

Father's Blessing to Speak Over Your Child

Dear child, may you see in your father a man worth imitating—someone whose words match his actions and whose character reflects God's heart. May the example he sets give you a clear picture of what it means to live with integrity, treat others with respect, and follow Jesus faithfully. And may you grow up wanting to be the kind of person your father has modelled for you. In Jesus' name, amen.

WEEK 32

Encouraging Their Curiosity

"Cry out for insight, and ask for understanding. Search for them as you would for silver; seek them like hidden treasures. Then you will understand what it means to fear the Lord, and you will gain knowledge of God."
— Proverbs 2:3-5 (NLT)

A Real Story

The theological questions started earlier than I expected. "Dad, if God loves everyone, why do bad things happen to good people?" "How do we know the Bible is true?" "What happens to people who never hear about Jesus?" These weren't simple bedtime questions—they were deep, complex issues that had challenged theologians for centuries.

My first instinct was to give quick, simplified answers or to deflect with "You'll understand when you're older." But I realized that approach would teach my children that faith questions weren't welcome or that doubt was dangerous. Instead, I started responding differently.

"That's a really good question," I'd say. "I don't have all the answers, but let's explore it together." We'd pull out the Bible, look up relevant passages, and sometimes even research what other godly people had said about the same question. I'd share my own struggles with similar questions and how my faith had grown through wrestling with difficult concepts.

What happened surprised me. Instead of becoming more confused or doubtful, my children became more engaged with their faith. They learned to study the Bible at a young age, not just read it. They discovered that asking hard questions actually strengthened their relationship with God rather than threatening it.

Biblical Reflection

Solomon encourages us to search for wisdom and understanding like hidden treasures, and this same passion for discovery should mark how we approach our children's spiritual curiosity. When they ask difficult questions about God, life, and faith, they're actually demonstrating the very heart Solomon describes—crying out for insight and seeking understanding.

Too often, we're tempted to shut down theological questions because we don't have perfect answers or we're afraid of saying the wrong thing. But our children's curiosity about God is actually a gift to be nurtured, not a problem to be managed.

When we explore difficult questions together with our children, we teach them that faith can withstand scrutiny and that God is big enough to handle their doubts. We show them that seeking truth is valuable, that intellectual honesty strengthens faith rather than threatening it.

Our willingness to say "I don't know, but let's find out together" models humility and demonstrates that learning about God is a lifelong journey, not a destination we reach in childhood.

Family Action Step

This week, when your child asks a difficult question about God, life, or faith, resist the urge to give a quick answer or deflect the conversation. Instead, lean into their curiosity with phrases like "That's a great question" and "Let's explore that together."

If your children are still very young, start creating an atmosphere where questions are welcomed by asking your own wondering questions aloud: "I wonder why God made flowers so many different colors," or "I wonder what it was like for Noah to trust God about the ark."

Keep a simple Bible handy for those moments when you can look up relevant passages together, showing your children that Scripture is the place we go to understand God better.

Reflection Questions

How do you currently respond to your children's difficult questions about faith, and what message does your response send about whether curiosity and doubt are welcome in your home?

What theological questions do you still wrestle with, and how might sharing your own journey of seeking understanding encourage your children's faith development?

Prayer & Blessing

Prayer for This Week

Father, thank You for my children's curiosity about You and about life. Help me to welcome their questions, even when I don't have perfect answers. Give me wisdom to explore difficult topics with them in age-appropriate ways, and help me to see their questioning as evidence of growing faith, not threats to it. Make our home a place where seeking truth is celebrated and where doubts can be safely explored. Teach me to model intellectual humility while pointing them always toward Your word. Amen.

Father's Blessing to Speak Over Your Child

Dear child, may your curiosity about God and life never be diminished but always encouraged. May you grow up knowing that asking hard questions strengthens faith rather than threatening it, and that your father delights in exploring truth with you. May you seek wisdom and understanding like hidden treasures, and may your search always lead you closer to the heart of God. In Jesus' name, amen.

Work and Family Balance:

Managing career and calling

WEEK 33

Working for More Than a Paycheck

"Work willingly at whatever you do, as though you were working for the Lord rather than for people."
— Colossians 3:23 (NLT)

A Real Story

The steady hum of the diesel engine and the endless stretch of interstate had become my world. As a long-haul trucker, I was making good money, better than I'd ever made before. The paychecks were substantial, and I convinced myself I was being a good provider for my family. After all, wasn't that what fathers were supposed to do?

But somewhere between Detroit and Chicago, during one of those long, lonely drives, I had a phone call with my wife that changed everything. She was telling me about our son's day, how he'd learned to ride his bike without training wheels, how he'd asked when Daddy was coming home, how he'd drawn a picture of our family but left my spot empty because "Daddy's always driving."

When I finally made it home after that two-week haul, I barely recognized the little boy who greeted me at the door. He seemed taller, older, and more independent. In the year and a half I'd been driving a truck, I'd been chasing a paycheck while my son's childhood slipped past me like mile markers on the highway.

That night, as I tucked him into bed and he asked me to stay until he fell asleep, I realized something profound: getting to know my son was infinitely more valuable than any amount of money I could earn on the road. I was working hard to provide for his future, but I was missing his present. The irony wasn't lost on me—in trying to be a good father through provision, I was failing to actually father him.

Within a month, I'd decided to leave the job for something more local. The pay cut was significant, but the investment in my relationship with my son was priceless.

Biblical Reflection

Paul's instruction to work "as though you were working for the Lord" transforms how we understand our role as working fathers. This isn't just about doing our jobs with integrity—it's about recognizing that our work serves a higher purpose than simply accumulating wealth or climbing the corporate ladder.

When we work for the Lord, we understand that providing for our families goes far beyond financial provision. Yes, we have a biblical responsibility to meet our family's needs, but we also have a calling to be present, engaged fathers who invest in our children's hearts and minds. The Lord we serve values relationships over riches, and when we work with this perspective, we make decisions based on what truly serves our family's best interests, not just their bank account.

The goal isn't to avoid hard work or to neglect our responsibility to provide, but to ensure that our work serves our family rather than consuming it.

Family Action Step

This week, have an honest conversation with your wife about your work-life balance. Ask her if she feels like your job is serving your family or if your family is serving your job. Listen carefully to her perspective and your children's needs.

Evaluate whether you're missing important moments for marginal financial gains, and consider ways to be more intentional about being present when you are home. If you're in a season where demanding work is necessary, make the moments you do have at home count by putting away devices and engaging fully with your children.

Reflection Questions

What does it mean to you personally to work "for the Lord rather than for people," and how might this perspective change your approach to career decisions and work-life balance?

When you look at your current work situation, are you primarily motivated by providing the best life possible for your family, or by personal ambition and the pursuit of more money or status?

Prayer & Blessing

Prayer for This Week

Lord, help me to work with the right heart and the right priorities. Show me how to be both a faithful provider and a present father. Give me wisdom to know when enough is enough financially, and courage to make decisions that truly serve my family's best interests. Help me to find purpose in my work by seeing it as service to You, and remind me that my children need my presence more than my presents. Guide me in creating a legacy of relationships, not just financial security. Amen.

Father's Blessing to Speak Over Your Child

Dear child, may you always know that you are more valuable to me than any paycheck or promotion. May you grow up understanding that true provision includes not just material needs but also love, attention, and presence. May you learn to work with purpose and integrity, always remembering that your greatest treasures will be the relationships you build, not the wealth you accumulate. In Jesus' name, amen.

WEEK 34

Protecting Family Time

"Then Jesus said, 'Let's go off by ourselves to a quiet place and rest awhile.' He said this because there were so many people coming and going that Jesus and his apostles didn't even have time to eat."
— Mark 6:31 (NLT)

A Real Story

When we decided to buy a 12-seater van, some people thought we were crazy. It was big, it wasn't fuel-efficient, and it definitely stood out in parking lots. But that van represented something important to us—the intention to create space for our entire family to experience life together.

We had committed early in our marriage that family time would be protected, and the van was part of that strategy. Road trips became legendary in our household. Whether we were driving to visit grandparents, heading to a family camp, or just taking a weekend adventure, that van was our mobile family room. The kids would pile in with games, books, and snacks, and we'd spend hours talking, singing, playing road trip games, and just being together.

Some of my most treasured memories happened in that van. Long conversations during highway stretches, impromptu sing-alongs, and the way our children learned to enjoy each other's company during those hours of shared space. It wasn't about the destination—it was about protecting time when we could just be a family, when work couldn't reach me, and nothing else could compete for our attention.

That van was more than transportation; it was a statement that our family time mattered enough to invest in, plan for, and protect from the countless things that could pull us apart.

Biblical Reflection

Even Jesus, with His divine mission and the urgent needs of people pressing in on every side, recognized the necessity of stepping away with those closest to Him. If the Son of God needed to create boundaries around His time and energy, how much more do we as fathers need to protect time for our families?

Notice that Jesus didn't just suggest rest when it was convenient—He initiated it when the demands were greatest. People were coming and going, ministry opportunities everywhere, and pressing needs all around. Yet He said, "Let's go off by ourselves." This wasn't selfishness; it was wisdom.

As fathers, we face constant demands on our time and attention. Work calls after hours, opportunities arise that promise advancement, and the culture around us suggests that being busy equals being important. But Jesus models a different way—one that recognizes the value of intentional time with those we're called to serve and love most.

Protecting family time requires the same kind of intentionality Jesus showed. It means saying no to some good opportunities to say yes to the best ones. It means creating rhythms and traditions that can't be easily disrupted by the urgent demands of daily life.

Family Action Step

This week, identify one regular time that will be protected as family time—whether it's Sunday mornings, Friday night dinners, or Saturday morning breakfasts. Communicate this boundary clearly to others and commit to protecting it from work interruptions or other obligations.

Plan one family activity that requires you to be fully present—whether it's a road trip, a hiking adventure, or simply a game night where everyone's phones are put away. The goal isn't elaborate activities but focused time together where your family has your undivided attention.

Reflection Questions

What messages are you sending your family about their importance based on how you currently protect (or don't protect) family time from work and other demands?

If Jesus felt the need to step away from His ministry to spend focused time with His disciples, what might this teach you about the necessity of creating boundaries around your family time?

Prayer & Blessing

Prayer for This Week

Father, help me to follow Jesus' example of stepping away from the urgent to focus on the important. Give me wisdom to know when to say no to opportunities that would steal time from my family, and courage to protect the time we have together. Help me to be fully present when I'm with my children, not distracted by work or other concerns. Show me how to create rhythms and traditions that will strengthen our family bonds and create lasting memories. Let my children always know they are a priority in my life. Amen.

Father's Blessing to Speak Over Your Child

Dear child, may you always know that you are more important to me than any job, any opportunity, or any obligation. May you grow up with memories of protected time when we were together, and may those moments teach you the value of prioritizing relationships over achievements. May you learn to create healthy boundaries in your own life that honor both work and family. In Jesus' name, amen.

WEEK 35

Learning from Other Dads

"As iron sharpens iron, so a friend sharpens a friend."
— Proverbs 27:17 (NLT)

A Real Story

I've been blessed throughout my life to have upstanding pastors who genuinely cared about my well-being. These weren't men who simply preached from a distance—they wanted to connect, to find out how I was really doing, and to invest in my life. What made their mentorship even more valuable was that they were all fathers themselves.

When I was struggling with how to discipline my children effectively, I didn't hesitate to ask one of them how he handled similar situations with his kids. When I was wrestling with balancing work demands and family time, I sought out another pastor who had successfully raised four children while serving in ministry. These conversations weren't formal mentoring sessions—they often happened over coffee, during car rides to church events, or in brief moments after service.

What struck me most about these men was their willingness to be honest about their own struggles and mistakes as fathers. They didn't present themselves as having all the answers, but rather as fellow travelers on the journey of fatherhood. One pastor once told me about a time he lost his temper with his son and had to apologize—that vulnerability permitted me to be imperfect while still striving to be better.

These relationships taught me that fatherhood was never meant to be a solo journey. The wisdom, encouragement, and accountability I received from these mentors shaped not only how I raised my children but also how I later sought to mentor younger fathers who came into my life. Iron truly does sharpen iron, and I'm grateful for the men who were willing to let their experience refine my approach to being a dad.

Biblical Reflection

Solomon's wisdom about iron sharpening iron reveals a fundamental truth about how God designed us to grow—through relationship with others who can challenge, encourage, and refine us. This principle is especially crucial in fatherhood, where the stakes are high and the learning curve is steep.

When we isolate ourselves as fathers, we miss out on the collective wisdom of men who have walked this path before us. We repeat mistakes that could have been avoided and struggle alone with challenges that others have already overcome. But when we seek out mentors and engage in meaningful relationships with other fathers, we tap into decades of accumulated wisdom and experience.

The sharpening process isn't always comfortable—iron striking iron creates sparks. Good mentors will challenge our assumptions, point out our blind spots, and hold us accountable to our calling as fathers. But this friction produces growth and refinement that we cannot achieve on our own.

Family Action Step

This week, identify one father whose parenting you respect and ask if you can buy him coffee to learn from his experience. Come prepared with specific questions about challenges you're facing as a dad. Don't be afraid to be vulnerable about your struggles—most fathers are honored to share what they've learned.

If you're a more experienced father, look for opportunities to invest in younger dads around you. Offer to share your experiences, both successes and failures, in ways that could help them grow in their fatherhood journey.

Reflection Questions

Who are the fathers in your life whose wisdom and example have shaped your approach to parenting, and how can you be more intentional about learning from them?

Are you currently trying to navigate fatherhood in isolation, and if so, what keeps you from seeking out mentorship or meaningful relationships with other dads?

Prayer & Blessing

Prayer for This Week

Father, thank You for the godly fathers You've placed in my life to learn from and be encouraged by. Help me to be humble enough to seek wisdom from those who have walked this path before me, and give me discernment to recognize the mentors You've provided. Make me teachable and open to correction, and help me to grow through the iron-sharpening-iron relationships You bring into my life. Show me how I can also be a source of encouragement and wisdom for other fathers who need support. Amen.

Father's Blessing to Speak Over Your Child

Dear child, may you always be surrounded by godly men who will invest in your life and help you grow. May you learn the value of seeking wisdom from those who have experience, and may you never be too proud to ask for help or guidance. May you also become someone who sharpens others through your example and encouragement. In Jesus' name, amen.

WEEK 36

Opening Your Home

"Don't forget to show hospitality to strangers, for some who have done this have entertained angels without realizing it!"
— Hebrews 13:2 (NLT)

A Real Story

It started with one child, then quickly became five, and later we added one more through the foster care system. People would often ask us how we managed with so many kids, but honestly, the chaos was just part of our normal. What they didn't expect was how naturally our home became a gathering place for even more children.

It was nothing for me to come home and find my kids' friends scattered throughout the house. Weekend sleepovers with 10 or even 12 kids were routine. Sleeping bags covering every inch of floor space, pizza boxes stacked high, and the sound of laughter echoing through the halls until late into the night. One of my favorite memories was when my son's entire graduating class decided to camp out in our backyard. We had tents everywhere, a bonfire going, and teenagers talking and laughing under the stars.

Our home had somehow become known as the safe place to go. Kids would show up not just for the fun, but because they knew they'd be welcomed, fed, and cared for. Some came from difficult home situations, others just needed a place where they could be themselves without judgment. We never set out to create this kind of environment. It just happened naturally when we decided our home would be a place of welcome rather than a fortress to protect.

Looking back, some of the most meaningful conversations I ever had with young people happened during those chaotic weekends. In the midst of all that beautiful mayhem, God was using our open door to touch lives in ways we never could have planned.

Biblical Reflection

The writer of Hebrews reminds us that hospitality isn't just about being nice—it's about creating space where God can work in unexpected ways. When we open our homes to others, we're participating in something sacred, something that can touch lives in ways we may never fully understand.

As fathers, we have the opportunity to model Christ's welcome by making our homes places of refuge and acceptance. This doesn't mean we abandon boundaries or wisdom, but it does mean we prioritize people over perfect order and relationships over pristine living rooms.

When our children see us welcoming others into our home, they learn that our faith is meant to be shared, not hoarded. They discover that hospitality is a form of ministry and that God often works through ordinary moments of kindness and welcome.

Family Action Step

This week, look for one practical way to make your home more welcoming to others. This might mean allowing your children to invite friends over more often, planning a family meal that includes neighbors, or simply creating an atmosphere where your kids feel comfortable bringing friends around.

Consider what barriers might be preventing your home from being a place of welcome—whether it's concern about mess, lack of preparation, or simply being too busy. Ask God to help you see your home through His eyes as a place where His love can be experienced by others.

Reflection Questions

What does your current approach to having people in your home teach your children about the importance of hospitality and welcoming others?

How might God want to use your home as a place of ministry and refuge for those who need to experience His love and acceptance?

Prayer & Blessing

Prayer for This Week

Father, help me to see our home not as my castle to protect, but as Your gift to share. Give me a heart for hospitality that welcomes others and creates space for You to work in their lives. Help me to prioritize people over perfection and relationships over convenience. Show me how to make our home a safe place where others can experience Your love through our family's welcome. Use our ordinary acts of kindness to accomplish Your extraordinary purposes. Amen.

Father's Blessing to Speak Over Your Child

Dear child, may you always know that our home is a place of welcome and safety, not just for you but for all who need refuge. May you grow up understanding that hospitality is a form of ministry and that God uses our open doors to touch lives. May you carry this spirit of welcome into your own future home, creating spaces where others can experience God's love. In Jesus' name, amen.

When Things Get Hard:

Faith for the difficult seasons

WEEK 37

Managing Your Anger

"And 'don't sin by letting anger control you.'
Don't let the sun go down while you are still angry."
— Ephesians 4:26 (NLT)

A Real Story

This isn't easy to admit, but I had an anger problem in my younger years. The pressures of work, finances, and the daily challenges of family life would build up inside me until I'd explode over something small. I told myself it was just stress, that every man dealt with frustration this way, but deep down I knew it was more than that.

The moment that changed everything happened during a particularly heated argument with my wife. I don't even remember what we were fighting about, but I remember the sound my fist made when it hit the kitchen table. In the silence that followed, I saw something in my wife's eyes that stopped me cold. Fear. Not just surprise or hurt, but genuine fear about what I might do next.

That look shattered something inside me. I realized that my anger wasn't just affecting me; it was creating an atmosphere of tension and unpredictability in our home. Our children were watching and learning that this was how men handled frustration. My wife was walking on eggshells, trying to manage my emotions along with everything else she carried.

I knew I needed to change, not just for my wife's sake, but for our children. They deserved a father who was safe, stable, and in control of his emotions. It took time, prayer, and sometimes professional help to learn healthier ways to process frustration, but it was one of the most important journeys I ever undertook as a husband and father.

Biblical Reflection

Paul's instruction about anger acknowledges something important—anger itself isn't sin, but what we do with it can be. Anger is often a secondary emotion that signals something deeper: hurt, fear, disappointment, or feeling out of control. The challenge for fathers is learning to identify what's really driving our anger and addressing it constructively rather than destructively.

When Paul says, «Don't let the sun go down while you are still angry," he's calling us to deal with our emotions promptly and directly rather than letting them fester and explode later. This requires developing emotional awareness and healthy outlets for frustration.

As fathers, our anger management directly impacts our children's sense of safety and security. Children need to know that home is a refuge, not a place where they have to monitor Dad's mood or worry about triggering an outburst. When we learn to handle our anger biblically, we create an environment where our families can flourish.

Family Action Step

This week, honestly assess how you handle anger and frustration. If you struggle with anger, take concrete steps toward change—whether that's talking to your pastor, seeking counselling, or finding accountability with other men. Your family's well-being depends on your emotional health.

Practice identifying your anger triggers and developing healthy responses before you're in the heat of the moment. This might include taking a walk, praying, or simply saying "I need a few minutes to cool down" before addressing the situation.

Reflection Questions

How does your approach to handling anger and frustration affect the atmosphere in your home and your family's sense of safety and security?

What are the deeper emotions or issues that typically fuel your anger, and how can you address those root causes rather than just managing the symptoms?

Prayer & Blessing

Prayer for This Week

Father, I confess that I don't always handle my anger in ways that honor You or serve my family well. Help me to recognize the warning signs before I lose control, and give me wisdom to address the deeper issues that fuel my frustration. Make me a safe harbor for my family, not a source of fear or unpredictability. Teach me to process my emotions in healthy ways and to model self-control for my children. Transform my heart and help me to be the steady, secure father my family needs. Amen.

Father's Blessing to Speak Over Your Child

Dear child, may you always feel safe and secure in our home, knowing that you are loved unconditionally. May you learn healthy ways to process your own emotions and never fear expressing yourself honestly. May you grow up understanding that real strength lies in self-control and that true men handle their anger with wisdom and grace. In Jesus' name, amen.

WEEK 38

When Plans Fall Apart

"We can make our plans, but the Lord determines our steps."
— Proverbs 16:9 (NLT)

A Real Story

It was supposed to be a perfect Saturday. We had two foster boys staying with us for the weekend, and I'd planned a special trip to the zoo with them and our son. I'd been looking forward to showing these boys a fun day out, hoping to create some positive memories and give them a glimpse of what family outings could look like.

The morning started well enough, but as we drove toward the zoo, the behavior in the backseat began to deteriorate. There was arguing, hitting, and deliberate defiance despite multiple warnings. I'd made it clear from the beginning that good behavior was expected and that if it continued, we'd have to turn around. I hoped it wouldn't come to that; after all, we were almost there, just about five minutes away from the entrance.

But as we sat at a red light with the zoo visible in the distance, I realized I had a choice to make. I could ignore the behavior and proceed with our plans, undermining my authority and teaching the wrong lesson, or I could follow through on what I'd said we'd do. My heart sank as I made a U-turn and headed home, watching the zoo disappear in my rearview mirror.

The disappointment was palpable, not just from the boys but from our own son, who had been looking forward to the day. Yet in that moment of turning the car around, something important happened. The foster boys learned that words have consequences, that boundaries matter, and that love sometimes means disappointing people for their own good. We had made our plans, but God determined our steps that day.

Biblical Reflection

Solomon reminds us of a fundamental truth about life—we can plan all we want, but ultimately God directs our path. This doesn't mean we shouldn't make plans, but it does mean we must hold them loosely and trust God's wisdom when circumstances require us to change course.

As fathers, we often face moments where our carefully laid plans must give way to what's best for our children's character development. These situations test whether we'll prioritize convenience and immediate happiness or stand firm on principles that serve our children's long-term good.

Sometimes the most important parenting moments happen when plans fall apart. These unscripted situations often reveal our true character and provide opportunities to model integrity, consistency, and trust in God's sovereignty even when it's costly or disappointing.

When we hold our plans with open hands, we teach our children that God's ways are higher than our ways and that sometimes the detour becomes more significant than the destination we originally intended.

Family Action Step

This week, when your family plans get disrupted or when you have to make a difficult parenting decision that disappoints your children, use it as an opportunity to discuss how God sometimes uses unexpected circumstances to teach us important lessons.

Practice holding your family plans loosely, being willing to prioritize character development and teaching moments over entertainment or convenience, even when it's difficult or disappointing in the moment.

Reflection Questions

How do you typically respond when family plans fall apart, and what does your reaction teach your children about trusting God's sovereignty in difficult circumstances?

Can you think of a time when a disrupted plan or disappointing situation actually led to an important lesson or outcome that wouldn't have happened otherwise?

Prayer & Blessing

Prayer for This Week

Father, help me to make good plans for my family while holding them with open hands, trusting that You determine our steps. Give me wisdom to know when to change course, even when it's disappointing or difficult. Help me to see disrupted plans as opportunities to teach important lessons about character, consequences, and trusting in Your sovereignty. Make me faithful in the small decisions so my children learn that integrity matters more than immediate happiness. Amen.

Father's Blessing to Speak Over Your Child

Dear child, may you learn to trust God's plan even when your own plans fall apart. May you understand that disappointments can become doorways to important lessons and that character matters more than comfort. May you grow up knowing that your father's love includes saying no when necessary and that God's steps for your life are always better than your own. In Jesus' name, amen.

Week 39

Financial Stress and Faith

"And this same God who takes care of me will supply all your needs from his glorious riches, which have been given to us in Christ Jesus." — Philippians 4:19 (NLT)

A Real Story

Raising six children has never been easy on the wallet, and honestly, it doesn't get much easier when they get older. While we no longer needed to buy diapers and formula, we faced new expenses. College tuition, car insurance for teenage drivers, wedding costs, and unexpected medical bills. There were seasons when I'd lie awake at night calculating and recalculating the budget, wondering how we'd make it all work.

As parents, we made countless financial sacrifices. We drove older cars longer than we wanted to, postponed home repairs, and chose family vacations that fit our modest budget rather than our dreams. I watched other families with fewer children enjoy luxuries we couldn't afford, and I'd be lying if I said there weren't moments of doubt and frustration.

But throughout all the financial stress and uncertainty, we made a decision that probably seemed foolish to outside observers. We continued to be generous with what God had given us. Even in our tightest seasons, we maintained our tithe, supported missionaries, and looked for opportunities to help families who were struggling even more than we were.

This wasn't always easy, and there were times when my wife and I questioned whether we should scale back our giving to ease our own burden. But each time we stayed faithful to our commitment to generosity, God showed up in unexpected ways. Through unexpected checks, timely job opportunities, or friends who blessed us just when we needed it most. Our children watched this process and learned that faith isn't just something you practice when it's convenient, but especially when it's costly.

Biblical Reflection

Paul's promise about God's provision isn't a guarantee of wealth or comfort—it's an assurance that God knows our needs and is faithful to meet them. This distinction is crucial for fathers facing financial pressure, because it shifts our focus from what we want to what we truly need and from our own ability to provide to God's faithfulness to supply.

Financial stress tests our faith in ways few other challenges do. Money touches everything—our security, our children's opportunities, our sense of adequacy as providers. When resources are tight, we're tempted to take matters entirely into our own hands, to compromise our values, or to become so focused on provision that we lose sight of the Provider.

The key to navigating financial challenges with faith intact is remembering that our role is to work faithfully and trust completely. We're called to be wise stewards and diligent workers, but ultimately our security rests in God's character, not our bank account balance.

When we model this kind of faith-filled approach to money, our children learn that God is trustworthy even in uncertain times and that generosity is an act of worship, not a luxury reserved for when we have extra.

Family Action Step

This week, have an honest conversation with your family about money that emphasizes both responsibility and trust in God's provision. If you're in a difficult financial season, look for one small way to demonstrate generosity or faith, whether that's maintaining your giving or helping someone in need.

Use current financial challenges as opportunities to pray together as a family and to teach your children that God cares about every aspect of our lives, including our material needs.

Reflection Questions

How does your approach to handling financial stress and making financial decisions reflect your faith in God's provision to your children?

In what ways might God be using your current financial situation to teach your family important lessons about dependence on Him and the difference between wants and needs?

Prayer & Blessing

Prayer for This Week

Father, thank You for Your promise to supply all our needs according to Your riches in Christ Jesus. Help me to trust in Your provision even when our finances feel tight and uncertain. Give me wisdom to be a good steward while keeping my ultimate security anchored in You, not in my bank account. Help our family to be generous even in difficult seasons, and use our financial challenges to draw us closer to You and to each other. Show my children through our example that You are faithful and trustworthy in every circumstance. Amen.

Father's Blessing to Speak Over Your Child

Dear child, may you learn to trust God's provision in every season of your life, whether abundant or lean. May you understand that your security comes not from money but from your relationship with the God who owns everything. May you grow up generous and faithful, knowing that God sees every sacrifice and honors every act of trust in Him. In Jesus' name, amen.

WEEK 40

Finding Joy in Hard Times

"Dear brothers and sisters, when troubles of any kind come your way, consider it an opportunity for great joy."
— James 1:2-3 (NLT)

A Real Story

Being the youngest of four children with three older sisters taught me the art of survival through humor. When the house got tense or when one of my sisters was having a particularly difficult day, I learned that a well-timed joke or a goofy face could shift the entire atmosphere. It wasn't that I didn't take serious things seriously. It's just that I discovered laughter could be a lifeline in stressful situations.

I've carried this tendency into my adult life and tried to pass it along to my children. When financial pressure mounted, when someone was sick, or when family tensions ran high, I made it my unofficial job to be the one who could find something to smile about. Not in a way that minimized real problems, but in a way that reminded everyone that joy was still possible even in difficult circumstances.

My kids have watched me crack jokes during hospital visits, find something funny to say when the car broke down on a family trip, and maintain a sense of humor even when work stress was overwhelming. I wanted them to learn that there should always be someone in the family willing to look for light in the darkness, someone who refuses to let hard times steal all the joy from our home.

Over the years, I've seen this approach take root in my children. During our toughest seasons, one of them would inevitably say something that made us all laugh, or they'd find a way to inject levity into a tense moment. They learned that finding joy in hard times isn't about denial. It's about resilience, and it's about choosing to believe that difficulties are temporary but family laughter can carry us through anything.

Biblical Reflection

James' instruction to "consider it an opportunity for great joy" when troubles come seems counterintuitive, but it reveals a profound truth about how God works in our lives. He's not suggesting we pretend hardships don't hurt or that we should be happy about suffering itself, but rather that we can find joy in what God accomplishes through difficult seasons.

As fathers, our response to trials sets the emotional temperature for our entire household. If we approach every difficulty with despair or anger, our children learn that hard times mean hopelessness. But if we can model joy even in the midst of challenges, we teach them that our circumstances don't define our outlook.

This doesn't mean we suppress real emotions or ignore genuine problems. Instead, it means we choose to look for God's presence and purpose even in painful situations. We find joy in how trials strengthen our character, deepen our dependence on God, and often bring our families closer together.

When we model this kind of resilient joy, our children develop emotional tools that will serve them throughout their lives. They learn that setbacks aren't permanent, that family can be a source of strength, and that laughter really can be medicine for the soul.

Family Action Step

This week, when your family faces a stressful situation or disappointment, look for ways to inject appropriate humor or find something positive to focus on together. This might mean sharing a funny memory, planning something to look forward to, or simply choosing to laugh together instead of dwelling on the difficulty.

Practice verbalizing what you're grateful for, even in challenging circumstances, helping your children develop the habit of looking for silver linings and reasons for hope during hard times.

Reflection Questions

How does your typical response to family difficulties affect the emotional atmosphere of your home, and what does it teach your children about handling life's challenges?

In what ways have past hardships actually strengthened your family's bonds or taught important lessons that wouldn't have been learned in easier circumstances?

Prayer & Blessing

Prayer for This Week

Father, help me to be a source of joy and hope for my family, especially during difficult seasons. Give me wisdom to know when to use humor appropriately and when to simply hold space for pain. Help me to model resilience and to show my children that You are present in every circumstance. Teach us to find reasons for gratitude even in our trials, and help our family to grow stronger through whatever challenges we face together. May our home be a place where joy can coexist with struggle. Amen.

Father's Blessing to Speak Over Your Child

Dear child, may you learn to find joy even in life's difficult seasons, knowing that troubles are temporary but God's love is eternal. May you develop resilience and the ability to encourage others when times get tough. May you always remember that laughter is a gift from God and that your family will be a source of strength and hope throughout your life. In Jesus' name, amen.

Creating a Christ-Centred Home:

Building family traditions that last

WEEK 41

Starting Family Devotions

"But as for me and my family, we will serve the Lord."
— Joshua 24:15 (NLT)

A Real Story

When our first child was just a few months old, my wife and I made a decision that seemed almost silly at the time. We started having family devotions. Here we were, reading Bible stories to a baby who couldn't even sit up, singing worship songs to someone more interested in chewing on his fingers than praising God, and praying together as a family of five where one member was likely to cry or need a diaper change mid-prayer.

Friends thought we were being overly ambitious. "Why not wait until he's older and can actually understand?" they'd ask. But we had a different perspective. We knew that as our children grew, the distractions would only multiply. School activities, sports, friends, technology, and countless other demands would compete for our family's attention. If we didn't establish the rhythm of worshiping together from the very beginning, it would become increasingly difficult to start later.

What began with simple picture Bible books and short prayers gradually evolved as our family grew. We added more children, and our devotion times adapted to include everyone from toddlers to teenagers. Some nights were chaotic, with little ones wiggling and older kids rolling their eyes, but we persisted because we understood something important: we were building more than just a spiritual habit—we were creating a family identity.

Biblical Reflection

Joshua's declaration, "as for me and my family, we will serve the Lord," wasn't just a personal statement—it was a family commitment that would shape how they lived, worshiped, and related to God together. This kind of intentional spiritual leadership requires fathers to take initiative in creating rhythms that center the family around God's presence and Word.

Starting family devotions isn't about perfection or elaborate programs—it's about consistency and creating space for God in the midst of ordinary family life. When we worship together regularly, we teach our children that faith isn't just a Sunday activity but a daily reality that shapes how we live.

The key to sustainable family worship is starting simple and staying flexible. A crying baby doesn't disrupt God's presence; it's part of the beautiful chaos of family life that God wants to sanctify. Young children may not understand every word, but they're absorbing the rhythm of seeking God together and learning that their family prioritizes spiritual things.

Family Action Step

This week, if you haven't already, start a simple family devotion time. Keep it short and age-appropriate—perhaps just reading one Bible story, singing a simple song, and praying together. Don't worry about perfection; focus on consistency and creating a relaxed atmosphere where everyone feels included.

If your children are older and you haven't established this tradition, don't be discouraged. It's never too late to start, though you may need to begin with even shorter, simpler formats and build gradually as the family adjusts to this new rhythm.

Reflection Questions

What specific steps can you take this week to begin or improve your family's worship time together, and what obstacles might you need to overcome to make this a consistent priority?

How might establishing regular family devotions now impact your children's spiritual development and your family's unity in the years to come?

Prayer & Blessing

Prayer for This Week

Father, help me to lead my family in worshiping You together, starting with simple steps that fit our current season. Give me persistence when it feels chaotic or pointless, and help me to see these moments as investments in my children's spiritual foundation. Make our family devotion times a source of connection with You and with each other. Help me to prioritize this rhythm even when life gets busy, knowing that You honor families who seek You together. Amen.

Father's Blessing to Speak Over Your Child

Dear child, may you grow up in a home where God's presence is welcome and His Word is treasured. May these early moments of family worship plant seeds of faith that will flourish throughout your life. May you always remember that our family serves the Lord together, and may this foundation guide you as you build your own family someday. In Jesus' name, amen.

WEEK 42

Praying Over Meals

"Since everything God created is good, we should not reject any of it but receive it with thanks. For we know it is made acceptable by the word of God and prayer."
— 1 Timothy 4:4-5 (NLT)

A Real Story

Our family devotions naturally evolved into a part of our nightly dinner routine, and along with that came the simple practice of praying before every meal. It started when our children were small—gathering around the table, holding hands, and taking a moment to thank God for the food before us and the day we'd shared.

What seemed like such a small thing became one of our most consistent family traditions. Whether we were eating at home, at a restaurant, or at someone else's house, our children knew that meals began with prayer. Sometimes it was a quick "Thank you, God, for this food" when we were rushing between activities, and other times it became longer prayers where we thanked God for specific blessings or asked for help with challenges we were facing.

As our children grew older and their schedules became more hectic, dinner time often became the only moment in the day when our entire family was together in one place. Those brief prayers before meals served as daily anchors. Reminders that no matter how busy life got, we were still a family that acknowledged God's provision and goodness in our lives.

I watched our children carry this habit with them as they grew up. When they went to friends' houses or later moved out on their own, they continued to pray over their meals. It had become such a natural part of eating that they couldn't imagine starting a meal without first acknowledging the God who provided it. Such a simple practice had quietly instilled a heart of gratitude that would serve them throughout their lives.

Biblical Reflection

Paul's instruction to receive God's gifts "with thanks" and through "the word of God and prayer" transforms something as ordinary as eating into an act of worship. When we pray over our meals, we acknowledge that every good gift comes from above and that even our daily bread is evidence of God's faithful provision.

This simple practice serves multiple purposes in family life. It creates a natural pause in our busy schedules, reminding us to slow down and recognize God's goodness. It teaches our children that gratitude should be our default response to God's blessings, not something we remember only during times of abundance or special occasions.

Meal prayers also provide consistent opportunities for family connection and spiritual formation. Unlike elaborate devotional programs that require special preparation, praying over meals happens naturally as families gather to eat together. It's accessible for every age, from toddlers who can fold their hands to teenagers who might otherwise resist family spiritual activities.

When we make thanksgiving a daily habit through meal prayers, we're training our hearts and our children's hearts to recognize God's presence and provision in ordinary moments.

Family Action Step

This week, if you haven't already established this practice, begin praying over every family meal—whether at home or away. Keep it simple and include everyone, even young children who can contribute their own words of thanks.

Use meal prayers as opportunities to teach gratitude by encouraging family members to mention specific things they're thankful for, not just the food, but also events from their day or blessings in their lives.

Reflection Questions

How might the simple practice of praying over meals together change your family's awareness of God's daily provision and develop hearts of gratitude in your children?

What does your current approach to meals and family time together teach your children about the importance of acknowledging God in ordinary, everyday moments?

Prayer & Blessing

Prayer for This Week

Father, help our family to see every meal as an opportunity to acknowledge Your provision and express our gratitude. Make our dinner table a place of connection, thanksgiving, and recognition of Your goodness in our lives. Help me to be consistent in leading our family to pause and thank You, even when we're busy or distracted. Use these simple moments of prayer to develop grateful hearts in all of us and to remind us daily that every good gift comes from You. Amen.

Father's Blessing to Speak Over Your Child

Dear child, may you grow up with a heart full of gratitude, always remembering to thank God for His daily provision. May the habit of prayer become as natural to you as breathing, and may you carry this practice of thanksgiving into your own family someday. May you never take God's goodness for granted but always recognize His faithful care in both ordinary and extraordinary moments. In Jesus' name, amen.

WEEK 43

Rest That Restores

"Then Jesus said to them, 'The Sabbath was made to meet the needs of people, and not people to meet the requirements of the Sabbath.'"
— Mark 2:27 (NLT)

A Real Story

Sunday afternoons became sacred time in our household, though it wasn't always that way. When I was driving a truck, weekends were often just another workday, and rest felt like a luxury we couldn't afford. But as our family grew and our involvement in church ministry increased, we discovered the life-giving power of intentional rest.

After the busyness of Sunday morning, church services, greeting people, ministry responsibilities, and the general chaos of getting everyone ready and out the door, Sunday afternoons became our family's sanctuary. We'd come home, change into comfortable clothes, and settle into what became an unspoken rhythm of rest.

Sometimes it meant everyone retreating to their rooms for naps, the house growing beautifully quiet except for the gentle sounds of people sleeping peacefully. Other times, we'd gather in the living room, reading books, playing quiet games, or simply enjoying each other's company without the pressure of productivity or schedules. The children learned that Sunday afternoons were for restoration, not for catching up on homework or tackling household projects.

What struck me most was how different everyone felt after these restful afternoons. The irritability that comes from constantly being "on" would melt away, replaced by a sense of peace and connection. We'd wake up from our naps or emerge from our quiet activities feeling genuinely refreshed, ready to face the week ahead. Those Sunday afternoon rests became as important to our family's well-being as any other tradition we established.

Biblical Reflection

Jesus' teaching about the Sabbath reveals God's heart for human flourishing through rest. The Sabbath wasn't designed as another burden or religious requirement to fulfill, but as a gift that meets our deep need for restoration and connection with God and family.

As fathers in a culture that glorifies busyness and productivity, we often struggle to embrace rest without feeling guilty. We worry that taking time to rest means we're being lazy or unproductive. But Jesus shows us that rest is actually essential for sustained effectiveness and emotional health.

Creating rhythms of rest for our families isn't just about physical recuperation—it's about creating space for souls to be restored. When we model healthy rest, we teach our children that their worth isn't tied to their productivity and that taking time to restore ourselves is wise stewardship of the bodies and minds God has given us.

Rest also creates natural opportunities for deeper connection within families. When we slow down and step away from the demands of daily life, we create space for conversation, reflection, and simply enjoying each other's presence without an agenda.

Family Action Step

This week, designate one regular time for family rest—whether it's Sunday afternoons, Saturday mornings, or whatever works with your schedule. Communicate to your family that this time is protected for restoration, not for catching up on tasks or activities that require energy and focus.

Create an environment that encourages rest by limiting distractions like television or demanding activities. Instead, focus on quiet, restorative activities that allow everyone to truly unwind and recharge.

Reflection Questions

How does your family's current rhythm of rest (or lack thereof) impact everyone's emotional health and your ability to connect meaningfully?

What barriers prevent your family from experiencing regular, restorative rest, and how might you remove or work around those obstacles?

Prayer & Blessing

Prayer for This Week

Father, thank You for designing us with a need for rest and for providing the gift of Sabbath restoration. Help me to lead my family in creating healthy rhythms of rest that restore our bodies, minds, and souls. Give me wisdom to protect these times from the demands of productivity and busyness. Help our family to find peace in slowing down together and to discover the deep satisfaction that comes from being rather than constantly doing. Make our rest times a source of connection and renewal. Amen.

Father's Blessing to Speak Over Your Child

Dear child, may you learn to value rest as a gift from God, not as something to feel guilty about. May you grow up understanding that your worth is not measured by your productivity but by God's love for you. May you find restoration in quiet moments and learn to create healthy rhythms of rest throughout your life. In Jesus' name, amen.

WEEK 44

Celebration and Worship

"Worship the Lord with gladness.
Come before him, singing with joy."
— Psalm 100:2 (NLT)

A Real Story

Through years of family devotions and regular church attendance, our home had become more than just a place where we lived. It had become a place where we could naturally celebrate and worship God together. The foundation of daily prayers and weekly worship had created an atmosphere where acknowledging God's goodness felt as natural as breathing.

Whether it was celebrating good grades from school, a successful job interview, or even something as simple as finding a lost toy after praying about it, our family had developed the habit of recognizing God's hand in both big and small victories. But some of my favorite celebration moments happened when one of our children shared how they'd been able to talk to someone else about Jesus—at school, with a friend, or with a neighbor.

I remember one particular evening when our teenage daughter came home excited to tell us about a conversation she'd had with a classmate who was going through a difficult time. She had been able to share how God had helped our family through similar struggles, and her friend had listened with genuine interest. We gathered in the living room that night, and instead of our usual devotional routine, we spent time thanking God for the opportunity and praying for her friend.

These moments of celebration and worship weren't forced or artificial. They grew naturally out of a family culture that recognized God's presence in everyday life. Our home had become a place where spiritual victories were just as worth celebrating as academic achievements or sports accomplishments, and where worship wasn't confined to Sunday mornings but could break out spontaneously whenever we recognized God's goodness.

Biblical Reflection

The psalmist's call to "worship the Lord with gladness" and "come before him, singing with joy" reminds us that worship should be characterized by celebration, not obligation. When we create homes where God's goodness is regularly acknowledged and celebrated, we teach our children that faith is meant to bring joy, not just duty.

Celebration and worship in the home doesn't require elaborate programs or perfect theology—it requires hearts that are quick to recognize God's hand in daily life and voices willing to express gratitude and praise. When our children see us celebrate God's goodness in ordinary moments, they learn that worship is a natural response to experiencing God's faithfulness.

Making our homes places of celebration also means creating an atmosphere where spiritual victories are valued alongside worldly achievements. When we celebrate our children's acts of faith, their kindness to others, or their growing relationship with God, we communicate what we truly treasure as a family.

This kind of celebratory worship creates lasting memories and shapes our children's understanding of what it means to live in relationship with a good and faithful God who deserves our joyful response.

Family Action Step

This week, look for opportunities to celebrate God's goodness in your home—whether it's answered prayers, acts of kindness your children show others, or moments when they demonstrate growing faith. Make these celebrations as enthusiastic as you would for academic or athletic achievements.

Consider establishing a family tradition of sharing weekly "God sightings"—times when you've recognized God's hand in your lives—and responding with prayer, gratitude, or even spontaneous worship through singing or praise.

Reflection Questions

How often does your family celebrate spiritual victories and God's goodness with the same enthusiasm you show for worldly achievements and successes?

What would it look like for your home to become a place where worship and celebration of God's faithfulness happen naturally and regularly, not just during crisis or formal devotions?

Prayer & Blessing

Prayer for This Week

Father, help our home to become a place where Your goodness is regularly celebrated and where worship flows naturally from grateful hearts. Give us eyes to see Your hand in both ordinary and extraordinary moments, and help us to respond with joy and thanksgiving. Make our family quick to celebrate spiritual victories and acts of faith, and let our children grow up knowing that serving You brings genuine joy and reason for celebration. Amen.

Father's Blessing to Speak Over Your Child

Dear child, may you grow up in a home filled with celebration of God's goodness and spontaneous worship of His faithfulness. May you learn that faith brings joy, not burden, and may you always be quick to recognize and celebrate how God works in your life. May worship and gratitude become as natural to you as laughter and love. In Jesus' name, amen.

Thinking Long-Term:

The legacy you‘re building

WEEK 45

Passing Down What Matters Most

"I remember your genuine faith, for you share the faith that first filled your grandmother Lois and your mother, Eunice. And I know that same faith continues strong in you."
— 2 Timothy 1:5 (NLT)

A Real Story

We all need someone to look up to spiritually, and I've been blessed to have a spiritual father who now serves as my spiritual director. His wisdom, guidance, and example have shaped my faith in profound ways. But if I'm honest, part of me always hoped it would have been my own father who passed down his faith to me in that intimate, intentional way.

My father was not a believer, and the spiritual inheritance I longed for didn't come through him. That experience taught me something important about the unique opportunity and responsibility I have as a father. I have the chance to give my children something that only I can provide: the faith heritage that comes from their dad.

For this reason, I've been intentional about making sure that what matters most. My faith is genuinely passed down to my children. Not just through Sunday church attendance or family devotions, though those are important, but through transparent conversations about how God has worked in my life, honest discussions about my struggles and victories, and consistent modelling of what it looks like to follow Jesus in everyday situations.

Biblical Reflection

Paul's commendation of Timothy's multi-generational faith reveals the power of spiritual inheritance passed from one generation to the next. The faith that "first filled" Lois and Eunice didn't stop with them—it became a living legacy that shaped Timothy's character and ministry.

This passage highlights both the privilege and responsibility we have as fathers to be intentional faith-passers. We have the unique opportunity to be the spiritual father our children look up to, the one who models what it means to follow Christ, not just in church settings but in real life with all its challenges and victories.

Passing down faith is different from passing down traditions or even biblical knowledge. It requires vulnerability, authenticity, and the willingness to let our children see not just our spiritual successes but also our struggles and dependence on God's grace. They need to witness faith that is genuine, tested, and lived out in practical ways.

The goal isn't to create carbon copies of our own faith journey, but to provide a foundation solid enough that our children can build their own authentic relationship with God—one that will sustain them through their unique challenges and enable them to pass something valuable on to the next generation.

Family Action Step

This week, have an intentional conversation with your children about your own faith journey, including both the victories and the struggles. Share specific ways God has been faithful to you and how your relationship with Him has grown and changed over time.

Look for opportunities to model authentic faith in everyday situations, letting your children see how you turn to God in both crisis and celebration, and how your faith influences practical decisions and responses to life's challenges.

Reflection Questions

What kind of spiritual inheritance are you currently passing down to your children through your example, conversations, and priorities, and how does it compare to what you hope they'll remember about their father's faith?

If your children were to describe your faith to their own children someday, what would you want them to say, and what changes might you need to make to leave that kind of legacy?

Prayer & Blessing

Prayer for This Week

Father, help me to be the spiritual father my children need and deserve. Give me wisdom to pass down genuine faith that is authentic, tested, and real. Help me to be vulnerable about my own spiritual journey while pointing them always toward You. May my children not just inherit my faith but develop their own vibrant relationship with You that will sustain them throughout their lives. Make me faithful in this sacred responsibility of spiritual inheritance. Amen.

Father's Blessing to Speak Over Your Child

Dear child, may the faith that fills your father's heart take root and flourish in your own life. May you build upon the spiritual foundation we're laying together and develop your own authentic relationship with God. May you someday have the joy of passing genuine faith on to the next generation, continuing a legacy of love for God that extends far beyond our family. In Jesus' name, amen.

WEEK 46

Stories That Shape Hearts

"We will not hide these truths from our children; we will tell the next generation about the glorious deeds of the Lord, about his power and his mighty wonders."
— Psalm 78:4 (NLT)

A Real Story

In our family, sharing faith stories became as natural as sharing news about our day. Whether it was during dinner conversations, family devotions, or quiet moments before bedtime, we made it a practice to tell each other about the ways we'd seen God work in our lives. Both in big, obvious ways and in small, everyday miracles.

These weren't formal testimonies or elaborate presentations, but simple accounts of how God had answered prayers, provided in times of need, or given strength during difficult moments. One of our children might share how they'd prayed about a difficult test and felt God's peace wash over them during the exam. My wife would tell about a perfectly timed phone call from a friend just when she needed encouragement. I'd share about how God had opened unexpected doors at work or provided wisdom for a challenging parenting situation.

What struck me was how these stories became sources of encouragement for the entire family. When one of us was facing a challenge, someone else would remember a similar situation where God had shown His faithfulness. The miracle one family member experienced became a learning moment for all of us, building our collective faith and creating a family narrative filled with evidence of God's goodness.

Over time, these shared stories became part of our family's spiritual DNA. Our children learned to look for God's hand in their daily lives because they'd grown up hearing story after story of His faithfulness to our family. They developed eyes to see miracles in ordinary circumstances because they'd been trained to recognize God's presence through the stories we shared.

Biblical Reflection

The psalmist understood something crucial about spiritual formation; faith is built through stories of God's faithfulness passed from one generation to the next. When we tell our children about "the glorious deeds of the Lord" and "his mighty wonders," we're not just sharing information; we're shaping their worldview and building their capacity to trust God.

Stories have power that abstract theology doesn't possess. When our children hear concrete accounts of how God has worked in their family's life, they develop a framework for understanding how He might work in their own circumstances. These narratives become reference points they can return to when their own faith is tested.

Sharing faith stories also teaches our children to be attentive to God's presence in daily life. When they know that their experiences of God's faithfulness will be welcomed and celebrated, they begin to look for His hand in their circumstances rather than dismissing coincidences or unexpected blessings.

The stories we tell shape not just our children's faith, but our family's identity. They create a sense of being part of a larger story of God's faithfulness that extends beyond individual experiences to encompass the entire family's journey with God.

Family Action Step

This week, make time to share faith stories as a family—either during a meal, family devotion time, or before bedtime. Encourage each family member to share a time when they saw God work in their life, answered a prayer, or provided what they needed.

Start keeping a family journal or create some other way to record these stories so they're not forgotten. Consider reading old entries occasionally to remind your family of God's continued faithfulness over time.

Reflection Questions

What faith stories from your own life could you share with your children to help them understand how God has been faithful to your family, and how often do you actually tell these stories?

How might regularly sharing stories of God's faithfulness change your family's ability to recognize His work in current circumstances and build confidence in His future provision?

Prayer & Blessing

Prayer for This Week

Father, help our family to become skilled storytellers of Your faithfulness and goodness. Give us eyes to see Your hand in both ordinary and extraordinary circumstances, and help us to be intentional about sharing these stories. Make these accounts of Your faithfulness sources of encouragement and faith-building for our entire family. Help our children develop the habit of looking for and remembering Your mighty works in their own lives. Amen.

Father's Blessing to Speak Over Your Child

Dear child, may you grow up surrounded by stories of God's faithfulness to our family, and may those stories build unshakeable confidence in His goodness. May you develop eyes to see His hand in your own life and a voice to tell others about His mighty works. May you become part of the next generation that refuses to hide God's truth but boldly shares His glorious deeds. In Jesus' name, amen.

WEEK 47

Building Memories with Purpose

"Remember the wonders he has performed,
his miracles, and the rulings he has given."
— 1 Chronicles 16:12 (NLT)

A Real Story

Over the years, I realized that all of our family traditions, whether daily, monthly, or annual, had developed a way of pointing toward God's faithfulness in our lives. Our birthday celebrations included prayers of thanksgiving for another year of life and God's blessings. Our vacation traditions involved family devotions in new places and conversations about how God had provided for the trip. Even our weekly routines, like Sunday dinners or bedtime stories, became opportunities to acknowledge God's goodness.

But I learned an important lesson about memory-making that changed how I approached these moments: while photos are important for preserving memories, stepping out from behind the camera and actually being part of those memories is even more important. I'd spent years documenting family moments while missing the chance to fully experience them myself.

I remember one particular Christmas morning when I was so focused on getting the perfect shots of the children opening presents that I realized I was watching their joy through a camera lens instead of experiencing it with them. That day, I put the camera down and joined them on the floor, wrestling with new toys and sharing in their excitement. The photos from that morning aren't as polished, but the memories are much richer because I was fully present.

Biblical Reflection

The chronicler's call to "remember the wonders" God has performed emphasizes the importance of intentionally preserving and reflecting on God's faithfulness. But true remembrance requires more than just documentation—it requires engagement, participation, and the deliberate creation of meaningful moments that point our families toward God's goodness.

When we build traditions with purpose, we're creating touchstone memories that will serve our children throughout their lives. These aren't just nostalgic moments, but spiritual markers that remind them of God's faithfulness to their family and His presence in both ordinary and extraordinary circumstances.

The key to memory-making that honors God is intentionality. We can transform routine activities into meaningful traditions simply by adding elements that acknowledge God's goodness, create space for gratitude, or provide opportunities for spiritual conversation and connection.

But perhaps most importantly, we must be fully present in these moments. Our children won't remember the perfect documentation of their childhood as much as they'll remember whether Dad was truly with them—emotionally available, engaged, and sharing in their joys and struggles rather than just observing from the outside.

Family Action Step

This week, identify one regular family activity or tradition that you can intentionally connect to God's faithfulness—whether it's adding a prayer of thanksgiving to birthday celebrations, sharing God-sightings during family meals, or incorporating worship into holiday preparations.

Practice being fully present during family moments by putting away distractions like phones and cameras when appropriate, choosing participation over documentation, and engaging with your children's experiences rather than just observing them.

Reflection Questions

How might your current family traditions and memory-making activities be enhanced by intentionally connecting them to God's faithfulness and goodness in your family's life?

When you think about your role during family celebrations and special moments, are you typically more focused on documenting the experience or fully participating in it, and how does that choice affect the memories being created?

Prayer & Blessing

Prayer for This Week

Father, help me to be intentional about creating family traditions and memories that point toward Your faithfulness in our lives. Give me wisdom to build meaningful moments that my children will carry with them as reminders of Your goodness. Help me to be fully present during these times, choosing participation over perfection and connection over documentation. Make our family traditions touchstones of faith that draw us closer to You and to each other. Amen.

Father's Blessing to Speak Over Your Child

Dear child, may you grow up surrounded by purposeful traditions that remind you of God's faithfulness to our family. May the memories we create together become treasures that strengthen your faith throughout your life. May you always remember not just what we did together, but how God was present in those moments and how deeply you were loved and cherished. In Jesus' name, amen.

WEEK 48

Praying for Their Future

"For I know the plans I have for you," says the Lord.
"They are plans for good and not for disaster,
to give you a future and a hope."
— Jeremiah 29:11 (NLT)

A Real Story

I've already shared about praying for our foster daughters, specifically that they wouldn't develop Huntington's disease. Prayers for health and protection over futures we couldn't control. But that was just the beginning of a lifetime pattern of interceding for our children's tomorrows, even when we couldn't yet see what those tomorrows would hold.

Today, our prayers for our children have evolved as they've grown. For some, we're praying about spouses they may or may not have met yet. Asking God to prepare their hearts for the right person and to guard them from relationships that would lead them away from Him. We pray for the character qualities they'll need to be good husbands and good wives. For wisdom in their career choices, and for their continued faithfulness to God through the challenges of adult life.

For the one who is already married, our prayers have shifted to include the future grandchildren we will eventually get to see and enjoy. We pray for their health, for godly homes to be established, and for the next generation of our family to grow up knowing and loving the Lord.

The point is, we have always been praying for their future, not just their immediate needs or current struggles, but for the people they're becoming and the lives they'll build. Sometimes these prayers feel abstract, interceding for people we haven't met and circumstances we can't imagine. But we've learned that our heavenly Father sees the full picture of our children's lives, and He invites us to partner with Him in prayer for plans and purposes that extend far beyond our current understanding.

Biblical Reflection

God's promise to Jeremiah reveals something beautiful about His heart for our children's futures—He already knows the plans He has for them, and those plans are good. This truth transforms how we pray for our children, moving us from anxious worry about unknowns to confident intercession based on God's faithful character.

When we pray for our children's futures, we're not trying to manipulate outcomes or force God's hand. Instead, we're aligning our hearts with His purposes and expressing our trust that He loves our children even more than we do. We're acknowledging that their lives extend beyond our ability to control or protect, but not beyond God's loving care.

Praying for unseen futures also shapes our perspective as fathers. It reminds us that our children's stories are still being written and that God is actively working in ways we may not yet see. This long-term view can help us navigate current challenges with hope and patience, trusting that God's plans for good will ultimately prevail.

These prayers also become spiritual investments in relationships and circumstances that may not materialize for years. We're sowing seeds of intercession that may not bear visible fruit until our children are married, have children of their own, or face challenges we can't yet imagine.

Family Action Step

This week, spend time specifically praying for your children's futures—their character development, their future relationships, their careers, and their continued faithfulness to God. Consider keeping a prayer journal dedicated to these long-term intercessions. If appropriate, share with your children that you're praying for aspects of their future they may not have considered yet. This can be encouraging and help them understand that their lives have purpose and direction even when they can't see the full picture.

Reflection Questions

What specific aspects of your children's futures do you find yourself most concerned about, and how might turning those concerns into regular prayers change your perspective and peace of mind?

How does believing that God has good plans for your children's futures affect the way you parent them through current challenges and decisions?

Prayer & Blessing

Prayer for This Week

Father, thank You for the promise that You have good plans for my children's futures. Help me to pray faithfully for the people they're becoming, the relationships they'll build, and the purposes You'll fulfill through their lives. Give me patience to trust Your timing and wisdom to support them through the journey. Help me to see beyond current challenges to the hope and future You have prepared. Make me a faithful intercessor for dreams and plans I can't yet see. Amen.

Father's Blessing to Speak Over Your Child

Dear child, may you always know that your future is secure in God's loving hands and that He has good plans for your life. May you walk confidently into tomorrow knowing that your father has been praying for you, your future spouse, your children, and the purposes God will fulfill through you. May you trust His timing and find hope in His promises. In Jesus' name, amen.

Celebrating the Journey:

Gratitude and looking ahead

WEEK 49

Counting Your Blessings

"Let all that I am praise the Lord; may I
never forget the good things he does for me."
— Psalm 103:2 (NLT)

A Real Story

As I look back on my years as a father, it's easy to focus on my mistakes. The times I lost my temper, the moments I was too busy to really listen, the opportunities I missed to teach important lessons. There's a natural tendency to replay the scenes where I fell short of the father I wanted to be, to dwell on the words I wish I could take back or the presence I wish I had offered more consistently.

But I've learned something important about reflection and memory: I need to consciously choose to look at the good things God has done through me as a father. Not because I'm perfect or because my mistakes don't matter, but because God has been faithful despite my shortcomings, and that faithfulness deserves recognition and praise.

When I intentionally count my blessings, I see how God provided wisdom in moments when I felt completely out of my depth. I remember conversations with my children that bore fruit years later, relationships that survived my imperfect parenting, and grace that covered over my failures. I see children who grew up to love God, not because I was a flawless father, but because God was faithful to work through my sincere but imperfect efforts.

Biblical Reflection

The psalmist's call to "never forget the good things" God does reveals an important truth about how we should evaluate our journey as fathers. While honest self-reflection is important, dwelling exclusively on our failures can blind us to the ways God has been faithful and generous despite our shortcomings.

When we count our blessings as fathers, we're not engaging in denial or minimizing areas where we need to grow. Instead, we're choosing to see our fatherhood journey through the lens of God's grace and faithfulness rather than through the filter of our inadequacies alone.

This perspective is crucial because it keeps us grounded in gratitude rather than regret, hope rather than despair. It helps us recognize that our children's positive qualities and spiritual growth are often the result of God's work through us, not just our own efforts or wisdom.

Counting our blessings also provides a foundation for continued growth. When we see how God has used our sincere efforts and covered our mistakes, we're encouraged to keep pressing forward in faith rather than being paralyzed by past failures.

Family Action Step

This week, take time to write down specific ways you've seen God's faithfulness in your journey as a father—moments when He provided wisdom, relationships that have flourished despite your imperfections, and evidence of His work in your children's lives.

Share some of these observations with your wife or a close friend, focusing on gratitude for God's goodness rather than pride in your own accomplishments. Consider how recognizing these blessings might encourage other fathers who are struggling with their own sense of inadequacy.

Reflection Questions

When you look back on your fatherhood journey, do you tend to focus more on your mistakes and failures or on God's faithfulness and the good things He has accomplished through you?

What specific blessings and evidences of God's grace can you identify in your children's lives that remind you of His faithfulness despite your imperfections as a father?

Prayer & Blessing

Prayer for This Week

Father, help me to see my fatherhood journey through the lens of Your faithfulness rather than focusing only on my failures. Thank You for the ways You have worked through my imperfect efforts and covered my mistakes with Your grace. Help me to count the blessings You have given through our family and to never forget the good things You continue to do. Give me a heart of gratitude that recognizes Your hand in my children's lives and celebrates Your goodness despite my shortcomings. Amen.

Father's Blessing to Speak Over Your Child

Dear child, may you always remember that your father's love, though imperfect, has been a reflection of God's perfect love for you. May you see how God has worked through our family's story, using even our mistakes for good. May you carry forward the blessings you've received and continue the legacy of God's faithfulness in your own family. In Jesus' name, amen.

WEEK 50

Milestones and Memories

"Samuel then took a large stone and placed it between the towns of Mizpah and Jeshanah. He named it Ebenezer (which means 'the stone of help'), for he said, 'Up to this point the Lord has helped us!'"
— 1 Samuel 7:12 (NLT)

A Real Story

We easily mark birthdays and anniversaries on our calendars, celebrating the passage of time and the natural milestones of life. But when it comes to moments when God has dramatically changed our lives, we don't typically mark those occasions with the same intentionality. We let these profound spiritual experiences fade into the background of memory rather than highlighting them as the life-changing moments they truly were.

However, our family has made it a point to talk about and commemorate different moments from our past when God showed up in unmistakable ways. Whether it was a mission trip that opened our eyes to God's heart for the world, a significant spiritual moment like baptism, or a time when God provided in an impossible situation, we've learned to make these experiences into milestones worth remembering and reflecting upon.

We'll sometimes pull out photos from a particular mission trip and talk about how that experience changed our perspective on serving others or sharing our faith. During family devotions, we'll revisit the story of someone's baptism and discuss what that decision meant and how it marked a turning point in their relationship with God. These aren't just nostalgic conversations—they're intentional efforts to build monuments to God's faithfulness in our family's story.

By regularly reflecting on these spiritual milestones, our children have learned to recognize and value the moments when God works in their own lives. They've developed the habit of seeing certain experiences not just as events that happened, but as stones of remembrance that mark God's help and faithfulness throughout their journey.

Biblical Reflection

Samuel's Ebenezer stone serves as a powerful example of how we should mark the moments when God shows up in our lives. This wasn't just a private memory or personal reflection—it was a public monument that declared God's faithfulness and served as a reminder for future generations of His help and provision.

As fathers, we have the opportunity to help our families establish their own "Ebenezer moments"—times when we intentionally mark and remember how God has intervened, provided, or transformed our circumstances. These spiritual milestones become reference points that strengthen faith during difficult seasons and remind us of God's track record of faithfulness.

The act of marking these moments teaches our children to be attentive to God's work in their lives. When they know that spiritual breakthroughs and divine interventions are worth celebrating and remembering, they begin to watch for God's hand in their circumstances rather than dismissing His work as a coincidence.

These milestones also become part of our family's spiritual heritage—stories that can be passed down to future generations as evidence of God's continued faithfulness to those who seek Him.

Family Action Step

This week, identify one significant spiritual milestone in your family's history and spend time reflecting on it together. This might be someone's conversion experience, a time when God provided in an impossible situation, or a mission trip that changed their perspective.

Consider creating a physical or digital "Ebenezer collection" where you document and preserve these spiritual milestones—perhaps through photos, written accounts, or special mementos that help you remember and retell these important moments.

Reflection Questions

What spiritual milestones in your family's history deserve to be remembered and celebrated as "Ebenezer moments" when God clearly showed up and helped you?

How might regularly revisiting and discussing these spiritual milestones strengthen your family's faith and help your children recognize God's ongoing work in their own lives?

Prayer & Blessing

Prayer for This Week

Father, help our family to recognize and mark the moments when You show up in our lives with power and faithfulness. Give us wisdom to create monuments of remembrance that will strengthen our faith and serve as testimonies to future generations. Help us to be attentive to Your work and intentional about celebrating the ways You help us. Make these spiritual milestones sources of encouragement and reminders of Your unfailing love. Amen.

Father's Blessing to Speak Over Your Child

Dear child, may you learn to recognize and remember the moments when God shows up in your life with help and provision. May you develop the habit of marking spiritual milestones that remind you of His faithfulness. May these monuments of remembrance strengthen your faith and become testimonies that you can share with the next generation. In Jesus' name, amen.

WEEK 51

Dreams for Tomorrow

"Then the Lord said to me, 'Write my answer plainly on tablets, so that a runner can carry the correct message to others.'"
— Habakkuk 2:2 (NLT)

A Real Story

Even though my children are all grown up now, I still carry dreams and hopes for my family's future. I look forward to the joy of walking my daughters down the aisle when they find the right person to marry, imagining those sacred moments when I'll place their hands in the hands of men who will love and cherish them. I even find myself dreaming about the possibility of meeting my great-grandchildren someday, even though I don't have any grandchildren yet.

These dreams might seem premature or overly optimistic to some people. After all, my children are still establishing their own lives, building careers, and figuring out their paths. But I've learned that there's nothing wrong with dreaming for tomorrow and allowing hope to fill my heart with anticipation for what God might do in our family's future.

These aren't just wishful thinking or idle fantasies—they're hopes rooted in faith and grounded in prayer. I dream about family gatherings that span multiple generations, about children and grandchildren who love the Lord and carry on the faith heritage we've tried to establish. I imagine holiday celebrations filled with laughter, traditions passed down, and new stories being written in our family's history.

Don't be afraid to pray into those dreams for your family's future. God has placed these hopes in your heart for a reason, and while His timing and plans may differ from your expectations, He delights in fathers who dream godly dreams for their children and their children's children. These visions of tomorrow give purpose to today's investments and remind us that our legacy extends far beyond our current circumstances.

Biblical Reflection

God's instruction to Habakkuk to "write the vision plainly" reminds us that godly dreams and visions are meant to be clear, purposeful, and shareable. When we have dreams for our family's future, we're not just engaging in wishful thinking—we're participating in God's desire to work through generations to accomplish His purposes.

Having dreams for tomorrow serves several important functions in our lives as fathers. It keeps us focused on long-term impact rather than just immediate concerns. It motivates us to make decisions today that will benefit future generations. And it fills us with hope and anticipation that can sustain us through difficult seasons.

These dreams also provide direction for our prayers and investments. When we can envision godly marriages for our children, faithful grandchildren, and a family legacy that honors God, we know what to pray for and how to prepare our children for the futures we hope they'll embrace.

But godly dreams are always held with open hands, submitted to God's sovereignty and timing. We dream boldly while trusting completely, hoping fervently while remaining flexible to God's better plans.

Family Action Step

This week, spend time writing down your dreams and hopes for your family's future—your children's marriages, their children, family traditions you hope will continue, and the spiritual legacy you want to see passed down through generations.

Share some of these dreams with your family in age-appropriate ways, letting your children know that you're praying and hoping for God's best in their futures while reassuring them that your love isn't conditional on these dreams being fulfilled exactly as you envision.

Reflection Questions

What specific dreams and hopes do you carry for your family's future, and how do these visions influence the decisions you make and investments you prioritize today?

How might sharing your godly dreams for your children's futures encourage them while also demonstrating your faith in God's plans for their lives?

Prayer & Blessing

Prayer for This Week

Father, thank You for the dreams and hopes You've placed in my heart for my family's future. Help me to dream boldly while holding these visions with open hands, trusting in Your perfect timing and plans. Use these hopes to guide my prayers, my investments, and my daily decisions as a father. Give me patience to wait for Your timing and faith to believe that You can do far more than I could ask or imagine for my family's legacy. Amen.

Father's Blessing to Speak Over Your Child

Dear child, may your future be filled with God's richest blessings, and may you fulfill the godly dreams He has planted in your father's heart. May you build a family that honors God, pass down a legacy of faith, and create new dreams that align with His purposes. May you always know that you are loved, prayed for, and believed in. In Jesus' name, amen.

WEEK 52

A Father's Prayer

"May the Lord bless you and protect you.
May the Lord smile on you and be gracious to you.
May the Lord show you his favor and give you his peace."
— Numbers 6:24-26 (NLT)

A Real Story

As we reach the end of this year-long journey together, I want to thank you for walking alongside me through these 52 weeks of reflection on fatherhood. My hope and prayer for you is that you don't think my life as a father has ever been perfect, because it hasn't been. I've shared victories and struggles, moments of clarity and times of confusion, decisions I'm proud of and choices I wish I could make again.

The truth is, I have simply done my best and allowed God to do the rest. That's been the consistent thread throughout my fatherhood journey. Sincere effort combined with complete dependence on God's grace, wisdom, and faithfulness. I've made mistakes that required apologies, faced challenges that drove me to my knees in prayer, and celebrated victories that I knew were far more about God's goodness than my own abilities.

What I've learned through raising six children, including those who came to us through foster care, is that perfect fathers don't exist, but faithful fathers do. Fathers who show up consistently, who pray earnestly, who love imperfectly but genuinely, and who trust God to work through their sincere efforts even when they fall short of their own expectations.

My prayer for you is the same prayer I have for my own children and grandchildren yet to come: that you would experience God's blessing and protection, that His smile would rest upon you, and that you would know His peace even in the midst of the beautiful chaos that is fatherhood. You don't have to be perfect; you just have to be faithful and let God handle the rest.

Biblical Reflection

The ancient priestly blessing that Moses recorded captures everything we need as fathers and everything we hope for our children. God's blessing and protection over our families, His gracious smile upon our efforts, and His peace that surpasses understanding—these are the gifts that sustain us through the journey of raising children who love and serve Him.

This benediction reminds us that our ultimate dependence is not on our own wisdom, strength, or perfection, but on God's favor and grace. As fathers, we can work diligently, pray fervently, and love deeply, but ultimately it's God's blessing that makes our efforts fruitful, and our families flourish.

The beauty of this blessing is that it's both for us and for our children. We receive God's favor and peace so we can be the fathers our children need, and we pray this same blessing over them as they grow and eventually become parents themselves. It's a legacy of grace that extends from generation to generation.

As you move forward in your fatherhood journey, remember that you're not alone. The same God who blessed and protected Moses' generation is present with you today, ready to smile upon your sincere efforts and fill your home with His peace.

Family Action Step

This week, pray the priestly blessing over each of your children by name, asking God to bless and protect them, to be gracious to them, and to give them His peace. Consider making this a regular part of your family's prayer time going forward.

Take some time to reflect on the past year of your fatherhood journey—both the victories and the challenges—and thank God for His faithfulness through it all, trusting Him with whatever the coming year may bring.

Reflection Questions

Looking back on this year of fatherhood, how have you seen God's blessing and protection over your family, even in the midst of imperfect parenting and challenging circumstances?

As you look ahead to the coming year, what hopes and prayers do you carry for your continued growth as a father and for your family's spiritual journey together?

Prayer & Blessing

Prayer for This Week

Father, thank You for the privilege of being a dad and for Your faithfulness throughout this journey. I confess that I am not perfect, but I trust that You can work through my sincere efforts and cover my mistakes with Your grace. May Your blessing and protection rest upon my family. Smile upon our home with Your favor, and fill us with Your peace. Help me to continue growing as the father my children need, and use our family to bring glory to Your name. Amen.

Father's Blessing to Speak Over Your Child

Dear child, may the Lord bless you and protect you as you continue to grow and mature. May His smile rest upon your life, and may you always know His gracious love and favor. May God give you His peace that surpasses understanding, and may you carry this blessing forward into your own family someday. You are deeply loved, thoroughly prayed for, and blessed beyond measure. In Jesus' name, amen.

www.ingramcontent.com/pod-product-compliance
Ingram Content Group UK Ltd.
Pitfield, Milton Keynes, MK11 3LW, UK
UKHW020726060126
9922UKWH00044B/890

9 789190 007211